If you've ever felt helpless, trapped—if you've ever longed for inner freedom—then the Old Testament books Exodus through Deuteronomy are for you. Today God invites you and me to travel with Israel down FREEDOM ROAD. In examining the history of another redeemed people, we can grow to a deeper understanding of our own redemption through Christ.

FREEDOM ROAD, a study of Israel's early days, takes us past what people say about the Bible and into what God is saying to us *through* the Bible.

LARRY RICHARDS

BIBLE ALIVE SERIES

Freedom Road

Understanding Redemption

Studies in Exodus, Leviticus, Numbers, and Deuteronomy

David C. Cook Publishing Co.

ELGIN, ILLINOIS—WESTON, ONTARIO
LA HABRA, CALIFORNIA

CONTENTS

FREEDOM ROAD

THEN . . . AND NOW

■ The Hebrew slave felt the flick of the lash; then the pain came. For a moment muscles corded in rebellion. But then he bent sluggishly to the task of mixing stubble with the slimy clay to be pressed into wooden forms for making brick.

■ *Virginia's head pounded. A headache always gripped her after a fight with Mom. Why did they fight? God knows she didn't want to fight with her. What was happening in their family? Virginia slumped helplessly on her bed, too defeated even to cry.*

■ It was the fear. Ruel couldn't bear it any longer. With tears in his eyes he carried the tiny body of his newborn son to the Nile, and, with a prayer to the ancient God of his ancestors, he obeyed the cruel command of this world's god, Pharaoh.

■ *"I didn't want to. . . ." It was like another person's voice.*

"I don't know why I went along with them. I guess . . . I guess I was afraid."

THEN . . . AND NOW

THESE ARE THE VOICES of people who are enslaved. People who struggle against bondage, but find themselves trapped. Wanting, but unable, to break free.

We need to start our study of Israel's journey down freedom road this way, with the realization that slavery isn't just something external. Bondage isn't something to which you and I are strangers.

That's what is so exciting about this adventure in the Old Testament books of Exodus through Deuteronomy. We'll be exploring our heritage from the past, yes. But as we do we'll discover a living heritage as well! In the Bible God speaks to men and women of every time and every place. He enters our *now*, and in His Word we not only discover the hope of ancient peoples; His Word brings us hope today.

This is particularly true for this important section of the Bible we'll be studying as we travel together down *Freedom Road*. Exodus, Numbers, Leviticus, and Deuteronomy record Israel's rediscovery of hope. The Hebrew people, the family of Abraham and Isaac and Jacob, had come to Egypt in the days of Joseph. They had settled on the west of the Nile's delta, an area called Goshen (present-day Cairo is on its southern end). Even after Joseph's death during the rule of Amenemhet III (about 1805 B.C.),[1] the Israelites experienced good years. Then, about 70 years after Joseph's death (about 1730 B.C.), a new people began a gradual conquest of Egypt. The country was ruled by a foreign aristocracy, the Hyksos, Semites from Asia. Goshen was one of the first areas conquered, and slavery was immediately imposed on Israel.

Later, when the Hyksos were driven out, Israel's lot was not easier. They had grown to be a numerous people. And they were more closely related to the Asiatic Hyksos than to the Egyptians! By the time of Thutmose I, Egypt's great empire builder, the presence of this foreign population seemed threatening. Thutmose's concern over a potential enemy at home while his armies were away seeking new conquests led to severe measures. He commanded Egypt's midwives to kill newborn Hebrew boys. When this failed, he directed all Egyptians to seize the male children that were born to Hebrews and fling them into the Nile to drown. Israel's plight was desperate.

And God acted.

This is why this study of Bible history can be so exciting for us. Sometimes our plight becomes desperate too. Sometimes we too are helpless, and can only call on God to act.

But what can God do? How does He work in our lives to lift us out of bondage and set us on the way to freedom? In the New Testament, looking back to the very days we'll be exploring, God tells us that

[1]Dates in this book are taken from *A Survey of Israel's History*, by Leon Wood (Grand Rapids: Zondervan, 1970).

13

the things that happened to Israel were "examples." The word "example" literally means "type"—a model or pattern. Israel's experiences were written down as signposts for us . . . signposts along a common road to freedom that we too are invited to travel (cf. I Cor. 10:11).

Simply put, *our personal experience with God closely parallels the experience of Israel as recorded in these Old Testament books!* These books show us how Israel was led from slavery to freedom. They tell us the great story of redemption, and help us understand what God intends to do in our lives as well. If you've ever felt helpless yourself, if you've ever sensed a need for inner freedom, then a study of these key books of the Bible is especially for you. For today God invites you and me to journey with Israel, down freedom road. God has acted in Christ to redeem you and me. Now, in examining the history of another redeemed people, He invites us to understand our own redemption.

WHY EGYPT?

It seems strange to realize that God led people He loved into slavery. But this is what happened to Israel.

God had appeared to Abraham, and had given him great Covenant promises. Abraham was to become a great nation. Through his offspring the entire race of man was to be blessed. And for the chosen people themselves there was to be God's own favor and protection. What's more, the family

14

was to inherit a land that, at the time, was a particularly rich one. Canaan was to be the Jewish homeland, a perpetual possession set aside for the favored family.

But after three generations (during which this Covenant promise had passed from Abraham to Isaac to Jacob) God led the 70 people of that family out of Canaan into Egypt. There, as God knew, they would rest and multiply—but would soon become enslaved. God's leading of the people of Israel into Egypt was unquestionably leading them into bondage.

Yet there were reasons for the detour into Egypt. During the years that the children of Israel lived in Egypt, the Promised Land was a battlefield. Invaders from the north, Hurrians and Hittites, had surged south. During the decades when Egypt's power was great, the Egyptian armies had flowed north. Palestine, a bridge between the two areas, knew the continual march of foreign armies, and often the devastation that war brings.

The Jewish people could hardly have multiplied or developed national strength in such a land.

But in Egypt the people grew. Scripture tells us they "increased abundantly, and multiplied, and waxed exceeding mighty; and the land was filled with them" (Ex. 1:7). Exodus 12:37 reports that when the Jewish people left Egypt, there were some 600,000 men, plus women and children; a total of at least two million people. Strikingly, when Israel left Egypt, both northern and southern world powers were weak. A power vacuum existed, which permitted time for the Jews to become established as a nation.

The geography of Palestine gives us another reason why the captivity was in God's plan for Israel. The land was divided by ranges of mountains and hills. In a similar land the Greeks developed a structure of independent and warring city-states. They had a common heritage, but lived divided lives. This could not be allowed to happen to God's people. Tribal distinctions would be retained, but the people must see themselves as one nation, linked forever by their common heritage in Abraham's God.

A third and striking reason for the time spent in Egypt is found in Genesis 15:16. In making the promise to Abraham, God told him that his descendants would be enslaved and oppressed in Egypt some 400 years. Following that experience of slavery, they would return. And then this puzzling note is added: "for the iniquity of the Amorites is not yet complete."

The Amorites were the people who lived in the land God had promised to Israel. Archaeological research tells us much about them—particularly about their depravity. They were a people whose moral and religious decline was marked by cult prostitution, and even involved the sacrifice of infants, who were burned alive to their nature gods.

For 400 years God, in grace, held back His judgment and permitted His own people to suffer. Only when the iniquity of the Amorites was complete— when they had reached a point of no return—did

God use Israel to judge and to destroy this depraved people.

And so for centuries Israel waited in Egypt. For centuries their suffering deepened. Only now, looking back, can we see the reasons. Even in their agony, God was working to do them—and others—good.

THE EXPERIENCE OF SUFFERING

These reasons for Israel's time in Egypt may fall short of the full explanation. This may be expressed in this simple report: "The people of Israel groaned under their bondage, and cried out for help, and their cry under bondage came up to God" (Ex. 2:23). It took the experience of suffering to lead Israel to cry out to God for help.

It's a peculiar thing, but it's true of most of us. When things are going well, we lose awareness of our need for God. Somehow we feel capable, in ourselves, to meet the challenges of life and of eternity. That feeling of need, that sense of helplessness which leads men to trust God, is lost. And in losing our sense of need we lose touch with reality.

The Bible is very blunt about reality. No comforting words are used to hide or distort truth. No wonder that Bible is not a very popular book with some people. While telling you and me that we are important to God, the Bible also tells us that our personalities are distorted by sin. We are both incapable of responding to God as He desires, and

17

unwilling to follow His ways. Sin, a warping within that twists our understanding and our desire and our will, stands as a barrier between us and the experience of God's love.

What seems to hurt us most is the warning that the barrier of sin is impenetrable from our side. In our pride we're willing to make up to God—but only if it is our efforts that scale the wall. We try. And we tend to ignore the warning that sin is something God must deal with.

That warning is never heard by many, many people. Or, if it is heard, it's resented and rejected. The reality of our helplessness is missed, as the illusion of adequacy clouds our insight. After all, we're competent to feed and clothe ourselves. We're competent to house our families. We're able to make our way in this world. We're certainly competent to judge right and wrong—we have consciences. And, if we don't *always* do what we know is right, at least we are morally a cut above others! As long as life goes on in its comfortable routine we remain trapped in the illusion of adequacy.

And then suffering comes.

Then we begin to experience our bondage.

Then the illusions begin to fade, and we glimpse the reality. We're forced to face the fact that we are creatures, trapped by circumstances over which we have no real control, and trapped by our own inability as well. Like Virginia, whom we read about at the beginning of the chapter, we realize that there's nothing we can do to break through the hostility and misunderstanding that destroy relationships. We realize that we are ruled by fear, forced by others into actions that we desperately want to avoid. By God's grace we may begin to groan under our bondage, and cry out. When we cry out to God, we rediscover hope.

Why was Egypt in Israel's experience? Why so many little Egypts for you and me? Perhaps so that God's people might never be deceived about their constant need for Him. The sense of helplessness that comes from an experience of bondage is often our first step down freedom road! You and I, as Israel, can never find freedom by looking within ourselves. We too need to look away, to God.

PREPARATION

The early chapters of Exodus give us fascinating insights into God's preparation to redeem. Behind the scenes, as Israel's sense of need deepened, God was already readying deliverance.

God's plan focused on Moses, a babe placed in the Nile (as the Pharaoh had ordered) . . . but resting in a floating basket of woven reeds. Moses was found by the daughter of Thutmose I, Hatshepsut. Captivated by the infant, she adopted him as her own. Afterward, when Moses was a youth, Hatshepsut seized power from a nephew who had been crowned Thutmose III, and ruled impressively for some 22 years. Moses, secure in the affections of this powerful and brilliant woman ruler, was well trained: "educated in all the wisdom of the Egyptians" (Acts 7:22).

When he was about forty, Moses was forced to make a choice. The burdens of his people Israel had grown greater during his lifetime. Finally Moses intervened and killed an Egyptian who was beating an Israelite slave. When he discovered that the killing had been observed, and when Thutmose III tried to kill him, Moses fled. No doubt this Pharaoh, who had resumed the throne after his aunt Hatshepsut's death (and immediately had ordered the defacing of all her monuments and the destruction of all records of her rule) was glad to find an excuse to remove his aunt's favorite.

Moses fled to Midian, a desert country far from Egypt, probably to the east of the present-day Gulf of Aqaba. There he lived for 40 years, his culture and his sense of pride gradually worn away by the simple life of the shepherd. Moses had abandoned his earlier vision of himself as his people's deliverer (cf. 2:11-15). Humbled by the experience, Moses was now a meek and therefore a *usable* man.

There must have been an urgency about God's desire for Israel's deliverance. But God took time to prepare Moses. Certainly the forty years in the wilderness was training in "desert survival," a skill Moses would later need. But even more, it must have taken the eroding of pride, until Moses became a man who would totally depend on the Lord when he returned to Egypt to renew his vision of a redeemed and freed Israel.

Dependent. It is easy in looking at Moses' call (Exodus 3 and 4) to misunderstand Moses' reactions. God called Moses from the burning bush, and stated His purpose of delivering His Covenant people from their sufferings. God promised to bring them to "a land flowing with milk and honey" (3:8). In fact, God gives Moses a whole series of great promises:

- "I have come down to deliver them" (3:8).
- The elders of Israel "will hearken to your voice" (3:18).
- While Pharaoh will not listen at first, "I will stretch out my hand and smite Egypt . . . after that he will let you go" (3:20).

Yet even with these promises, Moses hesitated and objected (4:1, 10, 13). Moses no longer saw himself as a competent man! Fully aware that he was unable to act alone, he was slow to realize that he *would* be able to act with God!

This is important for you and me to realize when we finally do recognize the reality of our own help-lessness and bondage. What we could not do alone, we *can do* with God! Sometimes we lose sight of God in the discovery of our own bondage and helpless-ness. The burning bush, and the promises of God, jolted Moses back to a full vision of reality. He hesi-tated . . . but finally Moses acted in faith. The bal-ance had been struck. Moses was now ready to trust God to do through him what Moses knew too well he could not do alone.

And this, ultimately, is reality.

We are helpless.

But God is not.

We are bound, but God is free. And in His freedom and power, He invites us to journey with Him down freedom road.

GOING DEEPER

to personalize

1. Is there an experience, or an area in your life, where you can identify with Israel as being "in bondage"? Can you briefly describe the situation and your feelings?

2. Draw a graph of Moses' life, showing its ups and downs, up to the point covered in Exodus 1—4. What do you think were the values of each peak and valley experience? Which direction do you think the graph line is about to take at 4:31?

3. Draw a graph of your own life, showing your ups and downs, up to today. What do you think were the values of your peak and valley experiences? What direction do you expect the graph line to take right now, as you look ahead? Why?

4. What statements of promise in Exodus 3 and 4 would be particularly meaningful should God speak them to you today? Why?

CONFRONTATION!

AT FIRST EVERYTHING seemed to be going so well. Moses' message of deliverance was believed by the elders of his people, "and when they heard that the Lord had visited the people of Israel and that he had seen their affliction, they bowed their heads and worshiped" (Ex. 4:31).

But the Pharaoh was different. When Moses and Aaron had their audience with the Pharaoh and asked only for a three-day journey into the wilderness to worship, the Pharaoh reacted quickly and brutally. An immediate demand for total freedom would have given the Pharaoh reason for such a rejection. God graciously laid on the proud ruler an easier command. The Pharaoh's reaction and its aftermath show only too clearly the character of the man Moses and Aaron faced. Enraged that his slave race dared think of even momentary relief from bondage, the king demanded that the Hebrews continue to meet their daily construction quotas, but now gather the raw materials that previously had been provided for them. When the quotas could not be met, the people were beaten.

Bitterly the leaders of the Jews accused Moses. Despairingly they pointed out that his request had "put a sword in their [the Egyptians'] hand to kill us" (5:21).

So Moses turned to God. In his own bitterness and despair, Moses asked "Why?" "O Lord, why hast thou done evil to this people? Why didst thou ever send me? Ever since I came to Pharaoh to speak in thy name, he has done evil to this people, and thou hast not delivered thy people at all" (Ex. 5:22, 23).

WHY?

For centuries now God's people had been slaves in a foreign land. But not in just any land; in Egypt. Egypt, with its mighty pyramids, developed culture, awesome temples, power and might and glory. Egypt, with its highly developed and complex system of worship, and with every material blessing constantly giving evidence of the ability of its gods to bless and protect the people.

In this land the Jews had lived as slaves for uncounted decades. Generation after generation had been born in slavery: over and over again, in countless ways, each child had been forced to realize that he was a member of a "subhuman" race. The jolting contrast between the cultured wealth of Egypt and the dull poverty of the slaves must have been a weight that pressed down continually on the Hebrews' sense of identity. Over the centuries all that gave these men and women any basis for a sense of pride and confidence had been eroded away. Yet, some retained a knowledge of God.

They told the old stories of God's appearance to Abraham, and they remembered the promises He had made. But those promises were made in a past which stretched twice as far back as our own struggle for independence! The fact that the Jews were to be plagued by idolatrous worship of Egypt's gods for many, many years after being reestablished in their homeland shows how deeply the "superiority" of the Egyptian way of life had impressed them.

Through these centuries of slavery the Jews had had no personal experience of God's power, and no new revelation. At best they must have had a hazy concept of who He was: a concept of a God who may have been powerful in the past, but who had not touched their present, nor the present of their fathers or grandfathers or great-grandfathers.

Finally, the years of slavery had culled imagination and courage out of the nation's men. Their slave mentality—often shown later on their wilderness journeys when they yearned for the onions and other vegetables of Egypt, and failed to value the freedom they had been given by God—had tended to be reflected in their leaders. Survival had demanded a passive, obedient people.

Now God would undertake to weld this family of slaves into a powerful nation. Now God would accept the challenge of rebuilding their personal and national identity: of remaking the slave into a free man. Now God would act to reveal Himself to Israel as a living God of the present, not merely a God of history. To accomplish these goals was no easy task. It demanded a dramatic demonstration of God's person and power. It demanded uncontrovertible proof of Israel's special place with the Lord. A quick surrender by the Pharaoh would have permitted Israel to avoid a certain amount of pain. But a quick surrender would have avoided the very confrontations through which God's greater purposes could be realized.

CONFRONTATION

God is a great dramatist. Now, in a series of striking confrontations, God acts out on history's stage a play which communicated, as words alone could not, the reality of His power and personal concern for Israel. It's helpful for us to read these chapters with the drama of these confrontations in view: to relive with the men and women of that time the identity of God and the identity of those on whom God sets His love.

Moses vs. Pharaoh. Moses' old enemy, Thutmose III, was dead. The new Pharaoh, Amenhotep II, was probably about 22 when confronted by the 80-year-old Moses. More than age contrasted when these two men met. There was a confrontation between life-styles and attitudes as well: a confrontation of meekness and pride. Moses had been 40 years in Egypt, nurtured as a somebody. For 40 years in the desert he had learned that he was a nobody. Now, as an earlier Bible teacher has pointed out, God would show what He could do with a somebody who was really willing to be a nobody.

Not so the young Pharaoh. In Egypt, society was structured around religion: a religion in which secular and sacred distinctions were lost, and the Pharaoh was himself considered a god. In official monuments the Pharaoh was often called *neter nefer*, the perfect god. We even have records in which a courtier describes Amenhotep II, this young man confronting Moses, as *neter aa*, the great god! Imagine then the pride of Amenhotep. Imagine Moses speaking in the name of the Lord God of Israel (God of slaves!). How easy it is to visualize the haughty pride that moves Amenhotep to respond, "Who is the Lord that I should heed His voice and let Israel go? I do not know the Lord, and moreover I will not let Israel go" (Ex. 5:2).

Through the succeeding judgments we watch the Pharaoh coming to know the Lord . . . and struggling against Him. At first the judgments fail to move him. Then, under the pressure of the supernatural, the Pharaoh promises to yield . . . only to return to his pride and obstinacy when a miraculous plague is removed. Even after the ultimate judgment, striking against his son and the firstborn of every Egyptian, Pharaoh changes his mind and sends his army to pursue a freed Israel.

In the confrontations between these two men, we

see in stark contrast the patience and steadfastness of faith against the backdrop of a self-exalting pride. It is the kind of pride which will not permit men to bow to God, even if it simply is for their own good.

Israel versus Egypt. One of the purposes expressed in the design of the plagues which God brought on Egypt was "that you may know that the Lord makes a distinction between the Egyptians and Israel" (Ex. 11:7). Anyone looking at the two peoples would have made a distinction between them. But not the distinction the Lord made!

The Israelites themselves were conditioned to evaluate . . . and to bow in shame before the culture and power of Egypt. Everything that men tend to value . . . the evidences of accomplishment, all the wealth, the education . . . were developed to a high degree in Egypt. Archaeologists still wonder at the mechanical feats of that people. Mathematicians and astronomers are amazed at the precise measurements that allowed great pyramids to mark with various architectural features the exact time of summer and winter solstices.

And the Israelites were slaves. Mere tools to be used by the master race, and tossed aside when they had served their purpose. Worthless. Poor. Subhuman. The Jews were beneath the notice of men.

But God made His own distinction between Egyptian and Jew! And God's value system is different than man's! God affirmed the worth and value of the slave people. In doing so, God not only kept the Covenant He had made with Abraham,

God also shouted out for all to hear that no man is "nothing" to Him.

We value what men *do.*

God values what men *are.*

The prophet Hosea beautifully reveals God's attitude, and helps us see that the distinction God put between Egypt and Israel was no mere legal act performed to honor a previous contract. It was that, but it was also an act of compassion, an act that flowed from love and concern for suffering.

> When Israel was a child, I loved him,
>   and out of Egypt I called my son.
>   . . . .
> it was I who taught Ephraim to walk,
>   I took them up in my arms;
>   but they did not know that I healed them.
> I led them with cords of compassion,
>   with the bands of love,
> and I became to them as one
>   who eases the yoke on their jaws,
>   and I bent down to them and fed them.
>   *Hosea 11:1-4*

The confrontation between these two peoples is important for us to see. We too are forced to choose between the value system each represents. We too are challenged to have compassion on the downtrodden of this world . . . and in compassion to reflect the character and the values of our God.

Jehovah vs. the gods of Egypt. This is the third, and the greatest, confrontation. We need to see these chapters of Exodus as a mighty struggle staged for our special benefit. In these chapters the God who *is* confronts all that which men call "god" but which is not. Dramatically, convincingly, God shows that He is victor over all.

Religion played a central role in the life of Egypt. Each of the many gods was seen as having control over vital aspects of the Egyptians' existence. Together, the structure focused on insuring a safe passage beyond this life into the next. Now, in a series of ten judgments, specific gods of the pagan pantheon were challenged by the Lord and defeated. The Pharaoh had asked, "Who is the Lord, that I should heed his voice?" Through the subsequent judgments, God announced, "The Egyptians shall know that I am the Lord" (Ex. 7:5). They would see His power, and His fame would spread throughout the earth (Ex. 9:16). What's more, the Jews would come to "know that I am the Lord your God" (Ex. 6:7).

In the plagues God would reveal Himself, and He announced, "On all the gods of Egypt I will execute judgments" (Ex. 12:12).

The first plague, the turning to blood of the floodwaters of the Nile, set the pattern for the others. To the Egyptians, the Nile itself was sacred. In its annual flood the river enriched Egypt's farmlands. The water from the Nile irrigated those narrow strips of fertile land on each bank which held and fed Egypt's population. No wonder this people of many gods dedicated hymns like this one, from the Middle Kingdom period, to the Nile:

30

Hail to thee, O Nile
that issues from the earth and comes to
keep Egypt alive.
He that waters the meadows which recreate,
in order to keep the kid alive.
He that makes to drink the desert and
places distant,
that is his dew coming down from heaven.

This Nile, that recreated life each spring, God at Moses' word turned rotten . . . polluted and stinking as spilled blood (Ex. 7:14-24). The source of Egypt's life died, and brought death. The gods of Egypt were powerless before the God of Egypt's slaves.

And so it went. The frog god of fertility, *Heka*, was represented in rotting piles of dead frogs. The god of the earth, *Seth*, was infested with lice, speaking to the Egyptians of ceremonial pollution. *Isis* and *Serapis*, gods of fire and water, were unable to protect Egypt from hail or locusts. *Ra*, the sun god, lost all power to overcome the blanket of darkness God threw over the land.

In each encounter, the gods of Egypt were judged, and found wanting. They went down in defeat before Jehovah the Creator God.

Bernard Ramm suggests that the confrontation of Jehovah and the gods of Egypt has even deeper significance. In God's judgments on Egypt, Ramm sees a confrontation "with all gods, power, authorities, principalities, and ideologies, visible or invisible, that oppose God and His truth and that

31

enslave and oppress men."[2] Whatever enslaves you, God can conquer, even as He conquered the empty gods of Egypt!

This is important to grasp. There is no power but God's power: *He* is the underlying reality. As you and I come to know Him, the powers that enslaved us will assuredly meet a similar defeat at His hand. The God who visited judgment on the gods of Egypt has the power to visit judgment on our captors too . And, because He is a God who has compassion, as we come to know and trust Him, He will.

THE MESSAGE

Many have pored over these significant chapters of Scripture, and noted exciting truths. These chapters are so full that it's all too easy to be distracted from the primary thrust.

The Pharaoh's hard heart. This question has been a favorite one for speculation. In some verses the Bible says God hardened Pharaoh's heart. In others Pharaoh hardened his heart. Do these phrases mean that God moved the Pharaoh against his will to sin? Was God the source of the Pharaoh's evil?

In Exodus 3:19 God tells Moses that He knows Pharaoh will not let Israel go unless compelled. Certainly Pharaoh's first reaction to Moses (Ex. 5) is a spontaneous one . . . one that gives us solid evidence that Pharaoh by nature is not responsive to

[2]Bernard Ramm, *His Way Out* (Glendale: Regal Books, 1974), p. 59.

32

God. Yet in Exodus 7:3, 4 God tells Moses that He will "harden Pharaoh's heart, and though I multiply my signs and wonders in the land of Egypt, Pharaoh will not listen to you." What is this hardening? And what does it all mean?

Explanations have varied. Some have pointed to the Hebrew approach to causation, which tends to trace responsibility back to God, ignoring intervening acts or choices by men. Others have suggested that God refers to the natural result of revelation: when God speaks to responsive hearts, they melt before Him. When God speaks to unresponsive hearts, they harden. Thus the same sun's growing heat melts wax, and hardens clay. Some have dismissed the whole debate as hinging on Hebrew idiom, and insist that the Jews did not mean by this phrase what it seems to mean in our tongue.

The Hebrew word used most frequently in this setting means "to be or become strong." Thus the derivation "to strengthen, to harden." We might paraphrase, perhaps, "God strengthened the Pharaoh's resolve to resist." This paraphrase would have one advantage. It would make perfectly clear that God did not force the Pharaoh to act against his own conscience or will. But even this would not resolve the question. God does say to the Pharaoh, "For this purpose I have let you live, to show you my power, so that my name might be declared throughout all the earth" (9:16). God could have acted differently than He did. Yet He let the Pharaoh, whose rebellion and mistreatment of Israel merited death, live. He let the Pharaoh live that he might be used by God for His own glory!

This is the fear that strikes at most of us when we read these chapters. It's not the theological issue of man's free will versus God's sovereignty. It is far more the emotional issue: the doubt and uncertainty that leads us to ask, "Is God the kind of person who will use me? Am I a pawn to Him, or does He care?"

The continual response of Scripture to this question is one of reassurance. Yes, God does care. He reached down in compassion to deliver Israel. He Himself stepped into our world . . . and was jerked upward on a wooden cross . . . because He does care. To all who respond with faith to His message of love, God commits Himself, even as He committed Himself to Abraham and Israel in a Covenant-oath.

But what of those who reject Him? Even here God is gracious. He does not immediately cut them off from the earth. . . . He shows them His power . . . and He "makes" even the wrath of men to praise Him. Looking back, Paul insists in Romans 9 that you and I recognize God's right to exercise compassion on men freely. All have deserved death. All choose freely . . . to sin. Yet in love God chooses to have mercy on some, and in others He strengthens the resolve sin has planted in the will. And we stand back in amazement, and realize that God is *God*. We can struggle to resolve this issue to our own satisfaction, and play our games with words to protect God's good character. But ultimately we have to admit that the resolution to this apparent paradox is beyond us. And we retreat, with joy, to the realization that the God who claims the right to exercise freely His own will is the same God whom we know in Jesus to be a God of love. Whatever choice God makes, whatever thing He does, will be righteous, and will be an expression of His love.

The miracles. Over a six-month span God brought a series of miraculous judgments on Egypt. These were recognized by Egyptian and Jew alike as God's special intervention . . . as "wonders" done by God's hand. Later speculation has grown about the nature of the miracles. Some have associated them with a volcanic cataclysm in the Mediterranean that destroyed what we have come to call "Atlantis," and the *Reader's Digest* has published serious articles explaining the relationship. Others have tried to explain away the miraculous elements by insisting these were merely normal occurrences, expanded by the storytellers. After all, locusts often infested that part of the world. The "bloody" Nile can be explained away by an unexpected infestation of algae. Even the death of Egypt's youth has been considered a sudden, but not unusual, childhood epidemic.

It is certainly probable that God did use natural events in the course of His judgments on Egypt. But the extent and the timing of these events made it very clear that they came by God's hand. On Moses' word judgments began; at his prayer they ended. Hail struck the Egyptians, but the Hebrew territories were free. The "childhood epidemic" struck only firstborn sons of families, and hit the entire land on a single night. And Hebrew children were strangely immune! No, to think that by suggesting "natural" events the miraculous element can be removed is to entirely miss the point.

Whatever means God chose to use, Egyptian and Jew knew that it was God who acted.

God known anew. As fascinating as is the speculation about the Pharaoh's hardening and the nature of the plagues, to focus on such issues is to miss the message of these vital chapters of Scripture. That message, what God was saying through these events to Israel and to us, is made strikingly clear.

We hear it in Exodus 6, as God says to Moses, "I am the Lord. I appeared to Abraham, to Isaac, and to Jacob, as God Almighty, but by My name the Lord I did not make myself known to them. . . . Say therefore to the people of Israel, I am the Lord, and I will bring you out from under the burdens of the Egyptians, and I will deliver you from their bondage, and I will redeem you with an outstretched arm and with great acts of judgment, and I will take you for my people, and I will be your God; and you shall know that I am the Lord your God, who has brought you out from under the burdens of the Egyptians."

It's important for us to realize what God is saying here. He is not saying that the name "the Lord" or "Jehovah" had never been applied to Him before. It had. He instead is saying, "You have not known Me as Jehovah." This is an important distinction. For the Hebrew, the word "know" spoke not only of casual information, but of intense and intimate personal experience. God tells His people, "You have heard the name Jehovah; now you will experience Me as Jehovah!"

This experiencing of God as Jehovah will be the key to all future relationship between Israel—and us—and the Lord!

What then does "Jehovah" mean, and why is it so special? The name itself is a form of the verb "to be," and is a proper name rather than an abstract term. "El" was the Semitic term for "God," and often appears in compound structures. Thus the Lord is sometimes described as "the God of battles," or "the God of our refuge." But God is never called "the Jehovah" of anything! "God" is His description. "Jehovah" is His name. In God's revelation of Himself to us as Jehovah we see a disclosure of His personal character and being.

What, then, does "Jehovah" imply? Simply that we are to see God as one who *is*. In fact, we might expand the thought communicated in this form of the verb "to be" and say that we now know Him as *"God who is always here."*

In this character, as a God of their present, the Hebrew people had not known the Lord! To Abraham, God had spoken promises about the future. So Abraham was always looking ahead, toward a time when God would break into the world of men to keep His covenant.

To the Jews in Egypt God was a God of the past. He had spoken to their fathers, but He had not spoken to them. Now, in a series of awesome

37

plagues and judgments, God was experienced by His people as someone who truly acted in their present.

The message was clear. To truly understand God you must see Him as someone who is with you now. What a revelation! And what a total revolution in Israel's thought. To begin to realize that God is not an event of past history or even a hope for the distant future, but someone with them now! Could it be? Could they live their present lives with confidence in a God with them now; with them to help them break out of their helplessness?

They could!

And we must.

We must, for the new vision of God given to Israel is the critical vision for anyone eager to experience redemption. Looking around us, at our inadequacies and at the circumstances that bind us, we are overwhelmed. Like Israel, the slave mentality grips us, and we surrender in our helplessness to the gods men erect. Our only hope then is to look away from ourselves and from our surroundings, and to catch a vision of our God as Jehovah. To realize that God wants us to experience Him as "the God who is always here." Because God *is* here . . . just as vitally here and now as He was here and now to Israel . . . you and I too have assurance of victory.

The God who judged the gods of Egypt and released His people from their bondage is with us today—to judge the empty gods that hold sway over you and me, and to set us free.

GOING DEEPER

to personalize

1. Read Exodus 5—11. If you were a Hebrew living in that day, how would you have experienced God as Jehovah, "the God who is always here"?

2. How have you experienced God's presence in your own life? Jot down several ways.

to probe

1. Select any two of the plagues described in these chapters and research their significance in view of Egyptian religion.

2. How did the judgments on Egypt affect different peoples? (Study Deut. 4:34; 7:19; Josh. 24:5; I Sam. 4:8; Ps. 78:43-51; 135:8, 9; Jer. 32:21.)

3. Explore the concept of "hardening" further. (A) First study the Biblical passages involved, not overlooking Romans 9. (B) Then look up at least three commentaries. (C) Finally, write briefly on how this topic relates to what the author suggests is the message of Exodus 5—11.

LIFE FROM DEATH

THERE ARE SOME DAYS no one forgets. Birthdays are eagerly anticipated when we're young; even as we grow old they can't be forgotten. Our birthday is important to us and to those who love us.

There are other days that have private importance, days we never want to forget, and which we mark off in special ways. I met my then wife-to-be on March 5, and still carry the slip of paper on which I wrote her phone number some 20 years ago. Whenever I go through my wallet I run across that slip of paper . . . and remember. Remember and relive the early days of that most joyful and painful of all relationships.

These chapters of Exodus have a similar importance. The events reported are in fact the birth of Israel as a nation. A special national feast, the Passover, is established to commemorate it. For Israel, recorded time begins here. The command to hold

Passover is the only divine legislation given Israel in Egypt, and the first sacrifice divinely ordained. It is one of only three festivals at which all Jewish males were later commanded to appear in Jerusalem for worship at the Temple. And, to date, it is the most explicit portrait of the cost of redemption.

THE PASSOVER

The ninth plague had fallen on the Egyptians. In a thick darkness that could be "felt," the Pharaoh had cried out in terror that Moses might lead the Israelites out . . . but that their possessions must remain behind. When this concession was rejected, anger overcame fear. The Pharaoh threatened Moses with death (Ex. 10:28). And the Lord told Moses that He was now ready to deliver the final stroke.

Following God's instructions, Moses moved the people to hurried preparation. They were told to ask jewels and gold from their Egyptian neighbors, and God would move them to give. They were to pack and prepare for a sudden journey. Bread must not be mixed with yeast—there might be no time to let it rise. The people must be ready to move instantly. Also, a young, unblemished lamb was to be taken into each household. It was to be kept for four days, then on the 14th of the month the lamb had to be killed, its blood sprinkled on the doorposts of the home, and the family within had to eat it, taking care to break no bone of the sacrifice.

42

But why should this ceremony be called "Passover"? Because on the night the lamb was slain, God's death angel would move through the land of Egypt. The firstborn son in every family, from the Pharaoh's own home to the home of the lowest servant, would die. Yet the death angel in passing through the land of Egypt would pass over the homes protected by the blood of the lamb.

God made a distinction between Egyptian and Jew. The lamb of sacrifice, the sign of the blood on the door, marked off God's people from all others. They alone were exempt from the decree of death.

The full significance of this event waited the coming of Christ. His death on Calvary took place as the Lamb of God, slain for the sins of the world. Yet the Old Testament believer could learn vital lessons.

■ *Relationship with God is a life or death issue.* Only identification with God's people as one of His exempted them from death.

■ *Redemption brings freedom at the cost of death.* Breaking the bondage of Egypt was not accomplished until the death penalty had been imposed. Israel's freedom was costly.

■ *Release from the death penalty is accomplished by sacrifice.* Somehow the blood of the sacrificial lamb covered and protected the household of the believing Jew. Later God would explain to this same generation: "The life of the flesh is in the blood; and I have given it for you upon the altar to make atonement for your souls; for it is the blood that makes atonement" (Lev. 17:11). Much later, the writer of the New Testament Book of Hebrews would see in *sacrifice* the necessity for Jesus' death: "Without the shedding of blood there is no forgiveness of sins" (Heb. 9:22). Sacrifice and forgiveness, the death of a substitute and spiritual freedom, would be forever linked.

Remembered. The importance of this first Passover is underlined by the divine demand that every year, without fail, the Passover experience be reenacted. Each year for seven days God's people were to commemorate their deliverance, "throughout your generations, as an ordinance forever" (Ex. 12:17). From the 14th through the 21st of Abib (Nisan, the modern Jewish equivalent of Abib, falls during March-April) the Jews were to eat no leaven. On the last night of the feast they were to take a lamb, kill and eat it. They were to eat the Passover meal standing, with their travel clothing on, and their walking staffs in their hands. And each year when the children asked, "What do you mean by this service?" the father was to respond, "It is the sacrifice of the Lord's passover, for he passed over the houses of the people of Israel in Egypt, when he slew the Egyptians but spared our houses" (Ex. 12:27).

Israel was never to forget its origin.

Israel was never to forget that it was a people delivered from slavery, and exempted from death. Israel was to remember, and yearly make the sacrifices that looked back to Egypt—and forward to the suffering Messiah.

Forgotten. It's fascinating to trace through the Old

Testament and note what happened to the Passover remembrance.

■ Numbers 9 tells us of the first anniversary experience, and of the special relaxation of ceremonial rules that make it possible for all of God's people to keep this unique feast.

■ Deuteronomy 16 repeats the command to keep the Passover, and adds that when Israel comes into the Promised Land the Passover is to be kept at the place where the Temple will be established. All the families of Israel are to come there and, if necessary, live in tents for the Passover week.

■ II Kings 23 tells of a revival under King Josiah, some 800 years after the Exodus, during which the Passover was reinstituted . . . after at least a 400-year lapse! The Hebrew people had forgotten redemption. In neglecting their beginnings, they had strayed from God into a series of deep spiritual and moral declines.

■ By New Testament times we see Passover carefully kept. In fact, we find the Passover week the focal point of each of the four Gospels. Matthew 21—28 reports the events of Passover week culminating in Good Friday and Easter. Mark 11—16, Luke 22—24, and John 12—21 (a good half of that gospel) all focus on that same Passover week. Why? Because it is here that the shadow cast by that first Passover is replaced by the solid reality it foretold. During this week Jesus Christ became our Passover Lamb and was sacrificed for us (I Cor. 5:7).

It is here that our freedom and our new life begin.

THE CENTRALITY OF SACRIFICE

It is important in looking at the Old Testament to realize that in it we see *acted out* realities that would be fleshed out later on. Even the details of the tent of worship were designed to reflect the pattern of heavenly realities (cf. Heb. 8:2-5). The entire system of sacrifices of the Old Testament, beginning here with the Passover lamb, are constant enactments of realities to come.

It's not hard to grasp why. When a young child is about to go into a hospital for a tonsillectomy, parents are often told to play "hospital" with him beforehand. For several days or weeks mom and dad rehearse the upcoming trip: they pack his bags, pretend to check in, look at pictures of hospital beds, take each other's temperature. In every way the young child is prepared, so that when he actually does enter the hospital it will all seem familiar. He will not fear, because the reality is so much like the pretend. Should we be surprised then that God took the same kind of care with us? That God planned for continuous enactments of reality, that when Jesus finally came to lay down His life for us, we would realize just what He was about? Should we be surprised at the centuries of animal sacrifice and the stress on the shedding of blood as necessary for forgiveness? No, in them we are led to understand that, to God, death has always been the price of new life for sinful men.

What should surprise us is that God would give His Son for us. That the blood spilled for us would be His own. But never should we be surprised that only the sacrifice of another's life can exempt one from the death penalty. Sacrifice has always been central in the history of God's gracious dealings with men. Over and over again the picture is presented to our eyes. Over and over again we see the blood. Over and over . . . until with awed amazement we look at Calvary and suddenly the pictures from the past merge into one. And we bow, stunned by the overwhelming reality.

He died.

For me.

Isaiah 53. Even in Old Testament days God lifted the veil to let us peek beyond the shadows at the reality. Isaiah 53 was long understood by the Jews to speak of the coming Messiah—the deliverer to be sent to them by God. In this passage we have a clear picture of Jesus . . . and of His sacrifice.

"Like a lamb that is led to the slaughter . . ."

"He makes himself an offering for sin . . ."

"He poured out his soul unto death . . ."

"He bore the sin of many . . ."

We can't read these words today without realizing that they contain God's explanation for Jesus' life, and for His death.

Hebrews 10. This chapter in the New Testament looks back on the Old Testament sacrifices from the perspective of the Cross. The sacrifices of old were "but a shadow of the good things to come instead of the true form of these realities" (10:1). The blood of bulls and goats could not take away sins (10:4). (The Old Testament word for the purpose of the sacrifices is *kaphar,* "to cover." The sacrifices covered sin and permitted God to overlook it until Jesus could come to *take sin away* by the sacrifice of Himself. Cf. Rom. 3:25, 26.) Yet what the old sacrifices foreshadowed, Christ accomplished! "By one sacrifice he has made perfect forever those who are being made holy" (Heb. 10:14). In Jesus our sins and lawless acts have been forgiven, and we have been cleansed. Thus "there is no longer any sacrifice for sins" (Heb. 10:18).

Today you and I look back on Calvary and mark it, as Israel did the first Passover, as the beginning of our lives as a freed people. We remember, as did the Jews, with our own ritual. But for us now the reminder is the bread and wine of Christian Communion. The Old Testament animal sacrifices had to be repeated over and over again as a constant reminder that sin, while temporarily covered, must still be dealt with. The repeated sacrifices served to demonstrate that no animal's life could ever satisfy the righteousness of God. The bread and wine of communion speak a different message! No longer is fresh blood required. Jesus has died, offering "for all time a single sacrifice for sins" (Heb. 10:12).

It is enough.

Redemption's work is done.

By the blood of Christ, you and I have been set forever free.

AFTERMATH

That first Passover accomplished its purpose, just

as Jesus' death accomplished its purpose, for all who trust Him.

But that night was a 'beginning, not an end. While the people were always to remember that "by strength of hand the Lord brought you out from this place" (Ex. 13:3), they were *not to remember in Egypt!* They were to leave immediately for the Promised Land.

Roundabout route (Ex. 13:17-22). The most direct route to Palestine was along the coast. But this would have thrown Israel into immediate conflict with powerful enemies. They needed time to learn to trust God. So God led them by a roundabout route, paralleling the Red Sea for about 100 miles southward down the Sinai Peninsula. Their journey brought them to the shore of a great body of water, in Hebrew called *yam suph*. This means, literally, "sea of reeds," and is probably best identified as the Bitter Lakes (see map). It was at this point, trapped against the waters and a dry wilderness, that Israel realized the Egyptians were pursuing them.

Deliverance (Ex. 14). The Pharaoh and the Egyptian people (vs. 5) recovered quickly. Perhaps the wealth Israel took with them motivated pursuit. At any rate, the Pharaoh set out to recapture his slaves, sending an army of 600 chariots on ahead. The Pharaoh himself followed the Israelites, and overtook them at the seaside.

But Israel, too, forgot all God's earlier acts! The people cried out bitterly against Moses, begging him to let them return to serve the Egyptians rather

FIGURE I

ROUTE OF THE EXODUS

than die in the wilderness. Moses' response makes a good watchword for us today: "Fear not, stand firm, and see the salvation of the Lord" (v. 13).

Redemption had been God's work. Deliverance of His people from each new peril would have to be His work as well.

We all know the story of the crossing of the sea. God opened and dried a path for His people. When the Egyptian army tried to follow, He brought the walls of water swirling back to destroy them. Perhaps we can imagine ourselves there, and realize what it must have meant to God's people to see their oppressors dead along the seashore. Perhaps we can sense the great release from fear, the joy of Israel at that moment. The Bible records it. Seeing what God had done for them, the people feared the Lord. And, finally, they believed.

The song. Chapter 15 concludes this section of Exodus with a record of the song the people of Israel sang, a song of joy and confidence and praise.

Like our own worship and praise, the song lifts up the person of God. It reviews what God has done. It raises up the fact that God truly is "One present with us!"

Redemption is the beginning of a relationship.

A relationship in which we are destined to *know* the presence, and the power of our God.

A TEMPTATION

In looking over these chapters of Exodus we face

51

a temptation to move into immediate and multiple application. The experiences of Israel are so suggestive of our own!

■ Israel was ready to leave. Aren't we called to leave the old ways of life when we come to know Christ? Are we to be as ready to abandon our past?

■ Israel left with all the riches of Egypt. Aren't we promised blessings forever more? Can't we too count on God to supply . . . richly?

■ Israel was to recognize redemption as God's act alone. Aren't we to look to Jesus as sole, and sufficient, Savior?

■ Israel was led away from an initial conflict which would be too much for the people. Doesn't God promise that He will not permit you to be tempted "beyond your strength"? (I Cor. 10:13).

We can become excited and carried away by a host of such correspondences between Israel's experience of redemption and our own. And there is value in this kind of analogy.

But let's never neglect the central message of redemption, portrayed so vividly in Israel's release. The Lamb must die that God's people can live. New life is purchased only at the price of blood. The sacrifice must be made to release men from the grim grip of death.

The Passover lamb played with the children of the Hebrew family, and they came to love it. It hurt them to see the lamb die. But their momentary pain was only an infinitely weak echo of the agony God Himself would feel when finally the time came to give His Son. This is the message of Passover.

Behold the Lamb.

Behold the Lamb of God.

It is He, the reality behind every sacrifice our Scriptures know, that we must see. Seeing Him, we know the great and freeing truth.

Our redemption is complete.

We're free now.

Free to set out on a journey to God's promised land.

GOING DEEPER

to personalize

1. Read through the Passover story (Exodus 11—13). Make a note of the similarities to Jesus.

2. In how many ways can you apply the experience of Israel in Exodus 13—14 to the experience of believers today?

3. Study the theme of sacrifice as it occurs in the Old and New Testaments. Focus your study on two passages mentioned in this chapter: Isaiah 53, and Hebrews 10. Be sure to *record in writing* everything you notice and learn.

4. Exodus 15 is a song of deliverance recounting Israel's experience with God. Try your hand at a personal "song of deliverance." Use the Exodus passage and its themes as a model.

to probe

1. It is popular in some circles to dismiss the doctrine of sacrificial atonement as an archaic and

outmoded concept. Explore this doctrine in one or more of the following ways:

(A) Read at least three discussions in different texts on theology, and write a summary report.

(B) Study, with a concordance, the Old Testament teaching on sacrifice, and write a summary report.

(C) Write a careful commentary on the argument of Hebrews 9 and 10.

(D) Use a concordance to examine all references to the blood of Christ and the Cross. Write up your discoveries.

2. The Passover itself is important in Biblical history. Learn everything you can about it, building from the Exodus text and considering all additional Old Testament and New Testament references.

DELIVERANCE AND DISCIPLINE

IN ATLANTA THIS PAST WEEKEND a young minister talked with me about his congregation. "So many of my people sit and wait for God to get folks down to the altar. And after a person comes . . . well, then everyone expects him to sit and wait some more till Jesus comes."

He was talking about people who misunderstood redemption. People who were looking at salvation as an end, not as a beginning. This is, of course, a lesson Israel had to learn, too. The song of rejoicing recorded in Exodus 15 is a shout of praise and release uttered by a people who suddenly realized that God actually had delivered them. Seeing the Egyptians dead on the shores of the sea, the Hebrews finally felt released . . . they knew that they were no longer slaves. They had been brought out of bondage! No wonder they shouted in joy:

> I will sing to the Lord, for he has
> triumphed gloriously;
> the horse and his rider he has thrown
> into the sea.
> The Lord is my strength and my song,
> and he has become my salvation.
>
> *Exodus 15:12*

As for people today, the realization of deliverance was an occasion for joy. Yet that song of praise soon turned to complaint. Israel's difficulties did not end at the Red Sea, any more than your difficulties and mine end when we trust Christ as Savior. For Israel, too, initial deliverance was not an end, but a beginning.

BEGINNING OF WHAT?

To put the happenings of Israel's next months and years into perspective, we need to shift for a moment to New Testament revelation. There we read about God's purpose for people today who come to know Him. The purpose is expressed in many ways, yet the thrust is always the same. Ephesians speaks of becoming "mature, attaining the full measure of perfection found in Christ" (Eph. 4:13, NIV). Romans speaks of being "conformed to the likeness of his [God's] son" (Rom. 8:29) and of being "transformed" (Rom. 12:1, 2). Colossians talks of putting on "the new self, which is being renewed in knowledge in the image of its Creator" (Col. 3:10). Peter insists that believers be like God (I

56

Pet. 1:14, 15), and explains his demand by pointing out that believers have "been born again, not of perishable seed, but of imperishable" or have, as J. B. Phillips paraphrases, "his [God's] own indestructible heredity" (I Pet. 1:23). Jesus Himself told His disciples they were to be "like your Heavenly Father" (Mt. 5:45-48).

The thrust of this line of teaching is clear. For the believer, salvation is the beginning of a process in which the individual is to grow in his likeness to Jesus Christ. Peter sums it up beautifully:

> But you are a chosen people, a royal priesthood, a holy nation, a people belonging to God, that you may declare the praises of him who called you out of darkness into his wonderful light. Once you were not a people, but now you are the people of God; once you had not received mercy, but now you have received mercy.   *I Peter 2:9, 10*

This same purpose sums up the calling of Israel. As a people who had received mercy, they were a chosen people belonging to God. Once a mob of slaves, they were now a nation destined to declare the praises of the Lord Jehovah who had called them.

In a few months Israel would stand before God at Sinai. He would teach them about their identity, claim them as His people, and announce:

> I am the Lord your God. Consecrate yourselves therefore, and be holy; for I am

holy. . . . For I am the Lord who brought you up out of the land of Egypt, to be your God; you shall therefore be holy, for I am holy.

Leviticus 11:44, 45

Israel must now learn to be like God! As a nation, they were called to reflect His character and His personality as a light to all men.

Yet the divine life-style which Israel was now called to learn was foreign to them. No wonder deliverance from Egypt was only a beginning. It was like being born again: born into a new world, called to learn new thoughts, new feelings, new attitudes, new values, and new behaviors. Only by seeing Israel's deliverance from Egypt as the birth of the nation—and tracing the subsequent events as God's training and nurture of a loved infant helped toward maturity—can we understand these next books of the Old Testament. Only then can we understand what they teach us about *our* own redemption.

THE CHILD

Exodus 15:22–17:7

Events immediately after the great deliverance show us how like a child Israel was. Looking back, it's no wonder the prophet Hosea uses the same simile:

When Israel was a child, I loved him,
and out of Egypt I called my son.

58

The more I called them,
the more they went from me;
they kept sacrificing to the Baals,
and burning incense to idols.
Yet it was I who taught Ephraim to walk,
I took them up in my arms;
but they did not know that I healed them.

Hosea 11:1-3

Squalling and willful, toddling off to grasp at forbidden "pretties," the infant Israel soon forgot the great acts of God through which it was delivered, and lapsed into complaint and a childish, willful bitterness.

Three days after crossing the Red Sea, the people were in a waterless wilderness, led there by God Himself through the agency of a cloudy, fiery pillar which was always visible to them (Ex. 13:21). When they did find water it was undrinkable, and the people "murmured against Moses." The Lord purified the water, and promised that if the people would be responsive and listen to His voice, He would continually be a "healer" to them (Ex. 15:22-26). Immediately after, God led them to Elim, an oasis with 12 springs and 70 palm trees, where they could rest from the desert journey and refresh themselves.

When they journeyed on, the people murmured against Moses again, complaining of hunger. The supplies they brought from Egypt had dwindled. God responded by bringing quail to the camp that evening, and in the morning produced the first of the *manna*[3] which would feed Israel all the time they were in the wilderness (Ex. 16:1-12). In spite of Moses' warning that their murmuring was against the Lord, and his warning not to gather more manna than they needed, the people "did not listen to Moses" (16:20).

Moving on by easy stages, Israel was again led to a place where there was no water. Panicked, they accused Moses of bringing them up out of Egypt to kill them with thirst. In their anger, they were about ready to stone Moses! But again God acted in grace to supply water, this time from a rock (Ex. 17:1-8).

What then is the picture we gain of infant Israel? It is a picture of people too immature to respond to grace; too willful to respond to guidance. God constantly demonstrated both His love and His ability to meet their every need. Yet in each crisis the people panicked and were unable to trust Him. Their response to pressure was more violent each time: they "murmured against Moses" (15:24); then "the whole congregation . . . murmured against Moses" (16:2); then "the people found fault with Moses" and "were almost ready to stone" him (17:2, 4). These people were not learning the divine life-style. They in fact rejected the first and most basic lesson: the lesson of trust. God had

---

[3]Manna was a waferlike substance appearing on the ground with the dew, tasting like honey and nuts. Only as much as could be eaten in a single day was gathered, except that the day before the Sabbath two days' supply was to be put in. On other days extra manna spoiled; on the Sabbath it did not.

proven Himself faithful over and over. Yet there was no awakening of response in the hearts or minds of His chosen people.

Israel proved itself to be a child.

INTRODUCTION OF THE LAW

Exodus 19, 20

We cannot understand the Ten Commandments and the Mosaic Law without realizing that they were given to Israel as a child. It was the infancy of Israel that made it necessary for God to introduce the Law.

Put in modern terms, we can look at the journey to Mount Sinai as a time when God dealt with Israel permissively. He let them respond naturally. He acted in love to meet their needs. He did not correct or punish. And the result demonstrated the outcome of all permissive approaches to child rearing. The people failed to develop inner discipline. They did not mature. They did not respond to God as a person, or delight in His purposes.

The Bible makes it very clear that God is not a permissive parent. And this section of Scripture shows us why.

Scripture tells us "the Lord disciplines him whom he loves, and chastises every son whom he receives" (Heb. 12:6. See also Prov. 3:11, 12). What's more, Scripture tells us the purpose of God's discipline: "He disciplines us for our good, that we may share his holiness" (Heb. 12:10). It takes discipline to develop holiness, and God will not shrink back from giving His children any good gift—no matter how painful that gift may initially seem!

It was because of love, then, and for the introduction of a discipline through which Israel might come to share His holiness, that God led the people to Mount Sinai. Love, and Israel's need for discipline, led to the giving of the Law. In later years the Law would be tragically misunderstood by God's people and distorted out of its divinely ordained role. But the Law was nevertheless necessary . . . for Israel.

A voluntary covenant. There is a striking difference between the Law Covenant, made at Sinai, and the covenant God made earlier with Abraham (Gen. 12, 15, 17). Then God had unconditionally announced what He intended to do. Now He proposed a mutually binding, and thus conditional, agreement. He reminded the generation coming out of Egypt of their deliverance; then He said, "*if* you will obey my voice" (19:5).

Obedience would bring blessing . . . the people would become "a kingdom of priests and a holy nation" (Ex. 19:6). But if that generation would not respond, and would continue in childish rebellion, they could not know blessing or represent Him.

Fear of the Lord. The events at Sinai now take on a striking appearance. The God who brought vast judgments on Egypt suddenly begins to thunder at Israel! Boundaries are set around the mountain, and no living thing is permitted to approach its slopes. A thick cloud covers the mountaintop;

thunder and lightning constantly play above the camp. Then, dramatically, a voice that stunned their senses spoke the now-familiar Ten Commandments to the gathered nation. The Bible tells us the "people were afraid and trembled; and they stood afar off, and said to Moses, 'You speak to us, and we will hear; but let not God speak to us, lest we die' " (Ex. 20:18, 19).

Awed and fearful, the willful people of Israel, for a time at least, were cowed. Psalm 111:10 says it: "The fear of the Lord is the beginning of wisdom." And Proverbs 1:7 echoes the thought: "The fear of the Lord is the beginning of knowledge." The child must learn to fear the parent before it can respond to love.

"The Law." Often in Scriptures "the Law" speaks of these first uttered commandments of God to Israel. But the word Law (*torah* in Hebrew), does not always refer to the Ten Words spoken from the mountain. It also refers at times to the whole system of life expressed by the continuing Old Testament revelation, a system containing many positive statutes and ordinances as well as the apparent negatives of the Ten. Also, the believing Jew thought of the books of Moses especially (that is, Genesis through Deuteronomy) as the Torah, "the Law."

But it is the Ten Commandments that draw our attention here, for these stand as the epitomy of the Old Testament Law.

Looking at them, remembering that Israel is a people who need discipline and training in holi-

63

ness, we're forced to ask, "Why these? What was God's purpose in giving Israel this Law, now?"

THE LAW

This first revelation of the Law to Israel performed two clear functions. First of all, it *revealed the character of God.* If Israel was to reflect God's character, and thus bring Him praise, they must understand His character! The Ten Commandments are our first sharp revelation of the character and the values of God.

Oh, we can infer much from earlier revelation: for instance, that God is faithful to His promises. But His moral character still remained something of a mystery. But no more. The Ten Words reveal the moral nature of this God who has taken it upon Himself to redeem a people to become like Him.

A second important function of the Law is that it *defines God's expectations.* In objective, clear, and well-defined standards, the people of God are told how He expects them to behave.

There is a tremendous value in any relationship in having expectations revealed. Some of us grew up in homes where we simply did not know how to please our parents. Nothing we did seemed to meet with their approval, and their commands to us would change from day to day. There was to be no such uncertainty for Israel in its relationship with God. God defined clearly the way He expected them to go, so clearly that even a child could not miss it.

With the limits established, and with God's expectations firmly expressed, the people would now be able to gauge their own responses and behaviors.

In modern terms this might be called an "immediate feed back system" ... something that is very important when anyone is being trained. For example, imagine a golfer practicing daily to eliminate a slice from his drive. He stands on the tee, swings and watches the ball ... adjusts, and tries again. He gauges each effort by watching that ball in flight, and, when he begins to straighten out the drive, he continues to practice to make sure that he has mastered the correct swing. Now, how much chance would the golfer have to improve if a screen were placed so he could tee up and hit, but not watch the ball's flight?

Obviously, without the feedback of seeing how he is doing, he simply could not correct his problem. In the same way, the Law provided an objective standard and served as a background against which the Israelites could obtain immediate feedback on their behavior. They could measure their plans, their goals, their values and their acts against the divine revelation of morality.

There are other functions of the Law as well, but these two help us begin to see its tremendous value to Israel at this point in its history. The Law would be for them a dual revelation: it would reveal the moral character of God, and it would show them themselves.

The Ten Words. What can we say about the content of this first moral revelation? Someone has suggested visualizing the commandments in terms of protection: protection of health in man's relationship with God, and the protection of health in man's relationship with other men.

How do the Ten protect man's relationship with God? First, we're taught that He alone is to be recognized as God (Ex. 20:2-3), and that He is to be worshiped in ways appropriate to His nature as Spirit (vss. 4-6). What's more, we are to forever affirm the meaningfulness of Jehovah's name as "One who is always Present" (vs. 7), and never take it as a vain ("empty") symbol. Finally, we are to build into the pattern of our lives a weekly reminder of God; a day of rest on which God's works of Creation, Rest, and Redemption, might be recalled as our daily tasks are set aside (vss. 8-11).

"Protection" also is a theme for the commandments dealing with interpersonal relationships. The parents' role (20:12), the sanctity of life (20:13), the institution of marriage (20:14), the right of property (20:15), the right to expect fair treatment from others (20:16), all provide protection for men in society. The final commandment goes far beyond all comparable law codes, and implies protection of the individual from himself. The prohibition against "coveting" strikes at the root of that which motivates us to violate the rights of others: it warns us to look within, and deal immediately with stirring motives which might lead us into sin.

As for external standards, then, the Law excel-

66

lently performed the functions for which it was designed. Looking to it, an Israelite could come to know his God and see in the words of the Law the divine heart of love, expressed as concern for the rights and integrity of each individual. And at the same time the Israelite could receive immediate feedback on himself. He could know, from the first stirrings within, to expression in action, any thought or behavior which was wrong.

For Israel, the fear of the Lord and the commandments of the Lord were truly vital . . . for their beginning.

GOING DEEPER

to personalize

1. How did believing Jews view the Law? Was it something that restricted . . . or freed? Was that a burden, or a joy? Look carefully at Psalm 19:7-10; Psalm 119:33-48.

2. Read Exodus 15:22-27, and trace the interaction between God and the Israelites. That is, jot down or chart His action, their reaction, His action, etc.

3. From your study (2 above), write up a one-page "character sketch" of the Hebrew people, as though the people were a single individual.

4. Examine the Ten Commandments themselves (Ex. 20:2-17), and from your study develop a list of God's values. (For the purpose of this assignment, define "values" as "what is important to" God.)

to probe

1. Many commentators have discussed the similarities between the Covenant of Law described in Exodus 19 and 20 and Hittite suzerainty treaties. Research in several texts to find out both the similarities and the differences reflected here.

2. The sixth commandment, "thou shalt not kill," reads literally "thou shalt not murder." Check Old Testament provisions both for the protection of those involved in accidental deaths, and the firm demand that those involved in premeditated murders be put to death. Do you find any difficulty in reconciling this command not to murder with the command to execute the murderer? If so, how do you resolve it?

3. Before reading the next chapter, do a research project on the New Testament view of the Law. Does it seem as universally commended as in the Old? How do you explain what you find?

THE BEGINNING OF WISDOM

TO MANY PEOPLE THE idea of the "Law" seems terribly restricting. Any expression of standards which are supposed to apply to everyone seems to them cold and impersonal. No wonder many with this viewpoint reject the whole idea of standards, and insist that "love" is enough! Thus, situation ethics, popular a few years ago, proclaimed that rules were unnecessary: that all a person needed was, in every situation, to determine the "loving thing to do."

There's something terribly tenuous about this notion. It's attractive all right. But how exactly does a person judge the "loving thing to do"? The situationist answer was: just look ahead and figure out the results of your possible choices, and select the course which will result in "good."

But how can you and I, fallible as we are, look into the future and know the results of our choices? Life is too complex. There are too many factors involved. Even with the best of intentions, we may be wrong.

Still, the situationist has a point. The Bible itself says that love does sum up the whole Law (Rom. 13:8-10). Love is at the very foundation of the Law, even as love is at the root of the restrictions and rules a good parent imposes on a toddler too young to know what is best for him. Strikingly, Scripture indicates that the very process the situationist suggests (looking ahead, and determining what is going to be best for the one loved) at least partially underlies God's reason for giving the Law.

For instance, Deuteronomy 15:4 promises that if Israel will only obey God's Law, "there will be no poor among you." The Law God gave to Israel was designed to produce justice and to eliminate injustice. In such a society, there would be no poor.

But there is a tremendous difference between you or me looking ahead and guessing at "the loving thing to do" without moral guidelines, and God looking ahead and knowing the loving thing for man to do. It is just because God does know the loving thing to do that He spoke out, and gave the Law to a people whose behavior proved that they were infants, desperately in need of guidance.

NO ABSTRACTS

Exodus 21–23

In our culture we're used to dealing with abstract ideas and concepts. "Love," for instance, is a term we like, yet one we're apt to misunderstand. If God had said nothing but "Love!" we might have been hard put to know what to do! But the Bible is practical. In Scripture God presents the abstract, but He then takes care to make sure it cannot be misunderstood. He provides multiple illustrations.

This is the best way to understand the "case law" we find in Exodus 21—23, following immediately after the Ten Commandments stated in Exodus 20. The great "Thou shalt nots" thundered from Sinai provided the framework for the moral life-style of Israel. They set the boundaries, showing the limits of the new life-style. Now, in the multiplied cases immediately following, God gives insight into the freedom provided *within* that framework!

What freedom?

The freedom this people had to love.

The freedom this people had to grow.

The freedom this people had to live in harmony with God and one another.

This is what we all really seek when we ask for "freedom." We want room to expand. We want freedom to become all we potentially are, and to do it without harming others or being harmed by them. This freedom, true freedom, is exactly what God provided for Israel within the framework of the limits established by the divine Law.

A positive life-style. The Ten Commandments provided a framework within which a positive life-style could be developed. The case law describes and illustrates that life-style, so that no one can miss the practical implications of the Ten.

71

What is that positive life-style like? Here are some examples:

†21:2 A Hebrew forced to sell himself as a slave shall be freed after six years.

†21:18, 19 A man injured in a quarrel is to be paid for the loss of his time and for required medical treatment.

†21:33, 34 A man leaving an open pit shall pay for another's animal that falls into it.

†22:1-4 A thief will repay what is stolen—and repay it at least double.

†22:16 A man seducing a virgin will marry her if the family of the girl is willing.

†22:21 A Jew shall not wrong a foreigner: the good law extends to strangers.

†22:26, 27 A man taking another's garment as a pledge for a loan shall let him have it nights; he may need to sleep in it for warmth.

†22:29 A man shall not delay to give God His offerings: God is to be first, always.

†23:3 In court, judges are not to be partial to the poor, but to consider only justice.

These are just a few of the examples in the Old Testament describing the freedom God intended to bring to His people through the Law. It was freedom too, because under this Law each person was protected from wrongs others might commit against him, and then was charged with a responsibility for others' welfare.

The Old Testament Law was given to Israel by a

loving God. Its very provisions constantly reveal that love, in action.

Cultural relevance. In reading the Old Testament, some have missed the spirit of love that infuses the Law. They have instead noted the fact that "slavery" was still permitted to God's people. They have been upset that the murderer is to be executed rather than "corrected." They have felt it unfair that women do not seem to stand as "equals" here.

How, they wonder, can such primitive moral codes as these passages reveal be considered a divine revelation—and how can they ever be understood as loving?

There are several answers to this kind of question; answers we need to consider carefully:

(1) *Whose standards do we accept?* Capital punishment is a good issue to illustrate this problem. It's popular today to decry capital punishment as an "inhumane" punishment, which brings the state down to the level of the murderer. "Forgiveness," we hear, "is a Christian virtue which supercedes the archaic vengeance motive of the Old Testament."

It's appropriate, though, to ask, "Who has the best and most accurate understanding of what is moral? Modern man—or God?" Certainly I would hesitate to affirm that my own moral judgment is more sensitive than His. If we do take seriously the notion that God might have moral insight beyond our own, it then seems appropriate to ask why capital punishment is instituted and stressed by Him. Is it really from a "primitive vengeance motive"?

Without belaboring the point, it seems that far

more than vengeance is involved. The prohibition against murder and the command to execute the murderer are first stated in Genesis 9:6.They are associated with the affirmation that man is made in God's image. Capital punishment is required, not as "vengeance," but as a necessary affirmation of the value and worth of human life. Where life is cheap in a people's eye, justice is impossible. There is no adequate response to murder but capital punishment, for there is no alternative way to affirm the ultimate value of the individual.

(2) *What world do we live in?* This question raises the issue of culture. The Jews of the Old Testament lived in their own time and culture—not in ours. In that culture slavery was part of life. The Old Testament Law guided the Israelites to live God's way in the world that existed then—not in the world that is today.

There is no doubt that freedom for all men under God's own rule is the divine ideal. But that ideal did not exist in the ancient world. The divine Law showed Israel how to express God's love in the real world. Strikingly, God's Law showed a compassion for slaves—and for women—foreign to the laws of other cultures. In both cases, persons disenfranchised by the culture because of their position were lifted up, and given new worth and value and rights by God's Word.

We might look for a modern parallel. You and I probably agree that the communist system is "less Christian" than the free-enterprise system. Does that mean, if we were living under communism, that we believers should commit ourselves to the overthrow of that way of life? Or does it mean that within the system we should seek to live Christ-honoring and Christ-revealing lives? I think the answer of Romans 13 is clear. We live, within our culture, a new kind of life marked by love for others that affirms the value of persons and, in a unique way, exposes God's own loving heart.

THE MOSAIC SYSTEM

We have seen, then, some of the uniqueness of the Law given by God to Israel at Mount Sinai. That Law was spoken to a nation in its infancy, a nation whose every response to the God who redeemed it from Egypt had been childish and harmful.

What the Law did for Israel was, first of all, to reveal something of the moral character of its God. Second, it specified very clearly God's expectations for Israel. The Jews now had a standard against which to measure their thoughts and actions.

But Israel had even more. In the Law Israel had been given the pathway to freedom and blessing. The way of living that the Law describes would bring the growth and joy which men have always longed for. Law guided Israel by defining clearly those responses to God and others that trust in God would stimulate them to make.

A conditional covenant. For all its benefits for Israel, the Law is a distinctly different kind of covenant than the early covenant with Abraham. And it is different from the later covenants, the one made with David and the New Covenant announced through Jeremiah.[4] These other Biblical covenants are unconditional. They are announcements of God's unchangeable purpose for His people.

But the Covenant of Law is a conditional one. At the very beginning, God had announced, "If you will obey my voice and keep my covenant . . ." (19:5). *The blessings promised under the Law depended on the people's obedience to it!*

Israel realized this. The generation that stood before Sinai accepted the condition, and responded, "All that the Lord has spoken we will do" (19:8).

After the Ten Commandments had been spoken, and the case law describing the life-style under the Law communicated, the people again expressed their willingness to enter into this covenant relationship with God. Even though they had been warned that disobedience and rebellion would bring punishment, just as obedience would bring blessing, the people still expressed their willingness to be bound in this relationship. "All the words which the Lord has spoken we will do" (24:3).

A mutually binding compact had been made. A compact in which, for the first time, God's commitment to act in the life of a particular generation was to be conditioned on their response to Him.

A basis for discipline. For God, this willing entry of His people into the Law Covenant provided a basis on which He could exercise necessary discipline. Before the Law wrong actions did not receive

[4]See *Let Day Begin,* chap. 8.

76

punishment, for such punishments would have no corrective value. When Israel knew what was right, and rejected God's guidance, punishment might teach them the importance of returning to His ways. As Hebrews tells us, God's chastisement is always purposive, always geared to stimulate our growth in holiness (Heb. 12:10).

An existential covenant. There is another very important thing to realize about the Mosaic or Law Covenant. Its focus is entirely on the present experience of each new generation of Israelites. This too stands in sharp contrast to the other Biblical covenants. The covenant to Abraham (Gen. 12, 15, 17) gave many promises, focused on a future time when the Jewish people would inherit the land of Palestine to the full extent that God intended. The promise to David (II Sam. 7) focused on the time yet future when the Messiah would sit on David's throne and reign forever. The covenant foretold by Jeremiah focused on a future time when Christ would die as its maker (Jer. 31), and a time yet future to that when all believers would be cleansed and transformed by His shed blood.

Thus the Biblical covenants are clearly statements of God's ultimate purposes.

But the Law Covenant says to living Jews, "If *you* will obey Me and keep My Law, then *you* will experience blessings. Now!"

A renewed covenant. The fact that the Law's purpose really was to determine the present experience of a given generation of Jews is shown in the way new generations are invited to "enter" that

77

covenant. One of Moses' last acts as leader of Israel is to call a new generation before the Lord and, setting the blessings and the cursings associated with keeping the Law before them, to invite them to "enter into the sworn covenant of the Lord your God, which the Lord your God makes with you this day" (Deut. 29:12). Still later, Joshua calls yet another generation to him, and demands, "Choose this day whom you will serve" (Josh. 24:15). And the people responded. They committed themselves to serve the Lord and obey His voice (Josh. 24:24). That generation too entered the Covenant.

Even to this day individual Jews agree to accept and abide by the relationship with God defined by the Mosaic Covenant. The infant is circumcised on the eighth day, indicating that his parents choose to bring him under the covenant with Abraham, and affirm his identity as a Jew. But then, at 13, each Jewish boy makes a personal decision. At his *bar mitzvah* (Aramaic for "son of the commandment") he repeats ancient words, accepts the obligations the Law spells out, and by his own choice commits himself to live under the rule of God's Law.

WHAT LAW IS . . . NOT

We can sum up the salient features of the Law as it is found in the Old Testament, then, by noting its functions in the life of Israel *and* by noting its differences from other Biblical covenants (see Fig. 2). We need to fix both considerations clearly in our minds. If we miss the unique nature of the Mosaic

FIGURE II

SUMMARY OF OLD TESTAMENT LAW

THREE KEY CONTRASTS

Other Covenants	*Law Covenant*
1. God only maker	1. Each generation/ individuals enter it with Him
2. Future in view	2. Present experience in view
3. Unconditional promise	3. Conditional, with promises and warnings

Law's Functions

1. To reveal God's character.
2. To reveal individuals to themselves in contrast to the pure standards of God.
3. To guide the believer's faith-response to God by specifying His expectations.
4. To provide a basis on which God can discipline His people.

Law we are all too likely to fall into the same errors which plagued later generations of Jews—and have warped the lives of many Christians as well. We are likely to misunderstand the nature of our redemption, the role of faith in salvation and in our subsequent Christian life, and even to miss the great contrast that exists between Law and Grace.

For Israel the giving of the Law, and the thunderings from the mount, instilled the fear of the Lord and marked a beginning of wisdom. But fear, and the Law, are only the *beginning* of wisdom. Both are later to be superseded by something far better that God has provided for us.

GOING DEEPER

to personalize

1. Jot down three rules you lived under as a child (or three rules you have for your children). Beside each, write its purpose, and how it (a) expresses love, and (b) provides freedom.

2. Read through either Exodus 21—23 or Leviticus 19, both of which are examples of Old Testament case law (that is, they illustrate with specific examples how the Law principles are applied). From your reading, select ten items and write briefly on each item (a) how it expresses love, and (b) how it provides freedom.

Try to pick several "easy" examples, and also to include several difficult items that will stretch you.

3. Imagine yourself to be an Israelite in the days of Moses. Imagine first that you truly do love God: how will you respond to the Law? Imagine then that you do not love God: how will you respond to the Law?

What does the difference in response tell you about the Mosaic Law and its limitations?

to probe

1. The author suggests that the Law gave God a

basis for discipline. Compare the following references and incidents. What does the different response God makes to similar incidents tell you? Exodus 32:25-35, and Numbers 11:1-21, 31-33 with Exodus 16:1-12. Numbers 15:32-36 with Exodus 16:23-30.

2. Without further study write a paper, limiting yourself to the Old Testament passages explored here, on "What the Law can and can't do." Write no more than three pages.

6

BEYOND THE LAW

IT MUST SEEM STRANGE, in view of the warm and positive view of the Law we've seen so far, to discover that the Law is only a temporary expedient—that in the New Testament God invites us to know something even greater, a freedom from sin's mastery that comes "because you are not under law, but under grace" (Rom. 6:14). Verses like this from the New Testament make it clear that we haven't yet come to know the full story of the Law.

In fact, the Law has often been misunderstood and misused. Unless we're careful, we too are likely to miss the blessing God has for us beyond the Law.

A WAY TO RIGHTEOUSNESS?

In the Law, Israel had a sharp and clear portrait of the moral character of her God. In the Law, men could see righteousness and love blend, and could understand God's commitment to do right by all persons. The Law's revelation of morality also served as a standard by which men could measure themselves. God had announced, "Be holy, for I am holy" (Lev. 11:44, 45). The Law's careful specification of holy behavior let men match their deeds to standards which God Himself had defined as right and good.

But when God's people did measure themselves against the Law, a striking message was heard. The men and women who had experienced redemption from Egypt discovered that they were not holy! The Law demonstrated their sin.

The events at Sinai themselves reveal the true character of Israel. Hearing God's voice of thunder, the people had cried out, asking Moses to mediate between them and this terror. For 40 days Moses talked with God on the mountain in his mediator role. While Moses was gone, the people of Israel insisted that Aaron make a golden idol, and in the very shadow of the awesomely burning, thundering mountain, they worshiped the idol as their god. They feasted before the idol, and "rose up" for immoral "play" (Ex. 32). Against the backdrop of the holy Law's beauty, the sinfulness of Israel could be clearly seen.

The Law, even when first given, did not produce righteousness. Instead it revealed man's unrighteousness. Through the Law men had the opportunity to discover their true state, to become conscious of the reality of their sin and need. This role of the Law continues today. It is stressed often in the New Testament. "We know," says Paul, "that whatever the law says, it says to those who are under the law, so that every mouth may be silenced and the whole world held accountable to God. Therefore no one will be declared righteous in his sight by observing the law; rather, through the law we become conscious of sin" (Rom. 3:19, 20).

Law, then, was never intended to produce righteousness. It was instead designed to help us see our need of forgiveness, and lead us to search out a righteousness through faith.

But this message was often missed. People came to the Law, but failed to see in it either God's heart—or their own. They missed the heartbeat of love that the Law reveals, and they treated it as a rule book. They treated the divine revelation as though it were a set of do's and don'ts through which a person might gain God's favor, and earn His approval by a man's own works.

Isaiah cried out against such a distortion of the Law's message, and against reducing righteousness to rule-keeping. In the Law, Isaiah reminds Israel, God has spoken and said:

> This is rest;
> Give rest to the weary;
> and this is repose;
>   yet they would not hear.
> Therefore the word of the Lord will be
>   to them
>   precept upon precept, precept
>   upon precept,

85

line upon line, line upon line,
here a little, there a little;
that they may go, and fall backward,
and be broken, and snared, and taken.

Isaiah 28:12-13

Men ripped the commandment from its context, and tried to build from God's revelation a system of regulations by which they might become righteous. Missing the heart and the function of the Law, they went and fell backward, and were broken and snared and taken.

When, in the letter to Titus, Paul wrote of God, "He saved us, not because of righteous things we had done, but because of his mercy" (3:5), the great Apostle was not adding to our knowledge of God. Salvation has always been God's gift, flowing from His heart of mercy. Salvation had never been based on "righteous things we had done."

Even father Abraham was accepted only because his faith was credited to him as righteousness (Gen. 15:6; Rom. 4). As Paul argues so strongly, and as every Jew knew, "It was not through law that Abraham and his offspring received the promise that he would be heir of the world, but through the righteousness that comes by faith" (Rom. 4:13).

No one who knew the history of Israel and the Old Testament revelation should have misunderstood this basic point. Righteousness comes through faith—not through the Law.

And yet many did misunderstand! Generation after generation tried to reduce the Law to a rule book, and righteousness to do's and don'ts. By their own efforts they struggled to develop (or to pretend) a righteousness which they simply did not possess. They refused to let the Law condemn them, that forgiveness might make them alive. And this mistake was fatal. "All who rely on observing the law," says Galatians 3:10, 11, "are under a curse, for it is written: 'Cursed is everyone who does not continue to do everything written in the book of the Law.' Clearly no one is justified before God by the law, because, 'the righteous will live by faith.' "

How clear it all seems. If you and I want to be righteous, we must look away from ourselves to God. But even today this truth gets obscured— because we as humans are basically self-centered.

God's perfect standards have shown us how imperfect and how at fault we are. If we admit our sin, we are free to surrender to God and to throw ourselves upon His mercy. If we are to become righteous, it must be through the work of God Himself in our lives, as we abandon ourselves and learn to live by faith.

A TEMPORARY FUNCTION

In neither Old nor New Testament is Law associated with righteousness. As Paul notes, "If a law had been given that could impart life, then righteousness would certainly have come by the law" (Gal. 3:21). But this has always been impossible.

Understanding this helps us realize that there is

no contradiction between Old and New Testaments when it comes to salvation. Some have thought that in early times people were saved (came into personal relationship with God) by keeping the Law, and later, after Christ, saved by faith in Him. No! It has always been a matter of faith. Law and Grace are not so different after all.

Yet there is a change between the Testaments as to one function of the Law. Law had a temporary Old Testament function which, according to the Bible, it no longer has since Jesus has come. To define that temporary function, let's look once again at what we've seen in these last chapters about the Law.

1. The Law always has revealed God's moral character.
2. The Law always has revealed righteousness and goodness.
3. The Law always has revealed sin, and underscored man's need for forgiveness and righteousness.
4. The Law never has shown man how to be saved.
5. The Law never has produced or provided righteousness.

Now we're ready to add one more fact.

6. The Law *at one time* was the avenue through which believers related to God.

We need to be very clear here. Obedience to the Law did not produce righteousness. Instead, *righteousness was expressed in obedience to the Law.* The person who truly trusted God (and who thus, as

Abraham, was declared righteous on the basis of his faith) demonstrated that inner transformation in obedience to the Law. We can diagram the relationships this way: (1) God spoke the Law. (2) The

FIGURE III

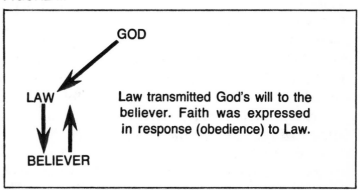

GOD

LAW

Law transmitted God's will to the believer. Faith was expressed in response (obedience) to Law.

BELIEVER

Law spoke to man. (3) The believer expressed his faith in God by seeking forgiveness through sacrifice, and then demonstrated the righteousness God has given him in obedience to the Law. In a very real sense the Law was a mediator between the believer and his God.

This mediator function of the Law was a temporary one. And it has been replaced by something better.

Galatians stresses the temporary nature of the Law's mediator function. "Now that faith has come [and through Christ we are sons of God], we are no longer under the supervision of the law," Paul argues in Galatians 3:25, 26. He goes on in chapter 4 to insist that the Law's old function as a pedagogue is no longer necessary. (A pedagogue was a slave who supervised the life of young children. The father gave the pedagogue instructions, and he saw to it that the children carried those instructions out. But when a child grew up, he became directly responsible to his father. No longer did the father relate to the child through the household slave. The slave was retired, his services no longer needed.) Paul's argument in Galatians is very clear. After Jesus came, and the Holy Spirit was sent into our hearts, the old relationship was superseded by something better. The coming of the Holy Spirit to live within the believer removes the necessity of relating to God through the Law.

In fact, in Galatians 5, Paul insists that we must live as men freed from this particular function of the Law if we are to experience all that Christ has provided for us. We are to learn that beyond the Law is a deeply personal relationship with God Himself in which "the only thing that counts is faith expressing itself through love" (Gal. 5:6).

Talk of the believer as no longer being "under the Law" frightens many people, who conclude that if a Christian can do "anything he wants" he will naturally want to do "anything." But this, of course, misses the whole point. The Book of Hebrews criticizes the Law system, saying that "the former regulation is set aside because it was weak and useless (for the law made nothing perfect), and a better hope is introduced, by which we draw near to God" (7:18, 19). Setting aside the Law's mediating function does not mean God is no longer concerned about righteousness. It simply means that God has a better way of helping believers grow in righteousness. In fact, the Bible promises that one who learns to live in response to the Holy Spirit's inner promptings will find that the "righteous requirements of the law" will be "fully met" in him (Rom. 8:4).

What then has changed? Let's look at another diagram:

FIGURE IV

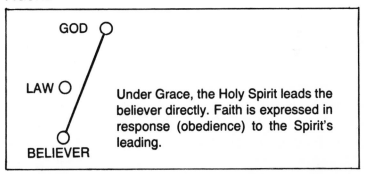

What has changed is that the believer is now related *directly* to God, without using the Law as a mediator. God the Holy Spirit will direct the believer's way, and will work His own inner transformation. God the Spirit will produce love, joy, peace, and patience—all those qualities of character which are in fact God's own.

God now commits Himself to work directly in our lives upon our character. The focus shifts from behavior in the Old Testament to the persons we are becoming in the New. And, as the Bible points out when it lists those fruits which the Holy Spirit produces in the believer's life, "against such things there is no law" (Gal. 5:22, 23). Law can add nothing to the life of a person who is truly like his Lord.

LAW VERSUS GRACE

In our survey studies of the New Testament we will see much more about the contrasting ways of life of the believer in the Old and New economies. For now, however, it is enough to realize that the Law was introduced in Israel's experience as a temporary expedient, to function as a mediator only until Jesus should come. Even while the Law was in force, however, it never replaced faith as a way of salvation. And it never was a means for producing righteousness.

Nonetheless, you and I have much to learn from the Law today. We learn about God. And we learn about our need. Yet when these two lessons have been learned, you and I are to turn away from the Law and turn directly to God. Paul talks of this when he insists that "sin shall not be your master, because you are not under law, but under grace" (Rom. 6:14). Freedom to relate to God, person to Person, is not freedom *from* the requirement of righteousness, but is instead *freedom to become righteous*.

God's Spirit within us, to teach and transform, is the One to whom we are to look. Never are we to think of relationship with God as something that can be summed up in lists of regulations. Never are we to look at our duty to our fellowman as something we can fulfill by following rigid sets of do's and don'ts. Instead we are to think of our spiritual lives as centered in a growing relationship with the person of Jesus Christ.

As we open up our lives to Him, the Spirit of God works to remake our personalities in His image. Now we are addressed by God as "renewed" men and women, "holy and dearly loved," and are invited to "clothe yourselves with compassion, kindness, humility, gentleness, and patience. Bear with each other and forgive whatever grievances you may have against one another. Forgive as the Lord forgave you. And over all these virtues put on love, which binds them all together in perfect unity" (Col. 3:12-14).

Do you see the difference?

The Law described righteousness in terms of behavior. Now Christ has come, and righteousness is described in terms of character.

The whole focus of the God/man relationship has changed. Never again dare we attempt to reduce righteousness to sets of do's and don'ts. In Romans 13:8-10, Paul says, "He who loves his fellow man has fulfilled the law. The commandments, 'Do not commit adultery,' 'Do not murder,' 'Do not steal,' 'Do not covet,' and whatever other commandment there may be, are summed up in this one rule: 'Love your neighbor as yourself.' Love does no harm to its neighbor. Therefore love is the fulfillment of the law."

If God has planted His very character in our hearts, and we reach out to men in His kind of love, we have no more need for the Law to show us what to do.

Freed from the Law, we stand forever free from the mistakes that plagued God's Old Testament people. We stand freed forever from the danger of reducing faith to rules from which the heart of love has been withdrawn. And we stand freed from the temptation to find in our *works* a righteousness which God says must dwell in our hearts.

GOING DEEPER

to personalize

1. In what ways today do you think Christians try to make Christianity into a "legal" system? Have you experienced the effects of this effort? How?

2. Select *one* of the several Bible passages listed below to study. Then write a one-page statement of "What this passage means to me." (Rom. 8:1-11; Gal. 3:1—4:7; Gal. 5.)

to probe

1. The Old Testament itself looks at the Law system as a temporary one, destined to be replaced by a new and better system which will in fact *produce* righteousness. To explore a key passage, write a three-page discussion of: *Jeremiah 31:31-34* (note, see use of this passage in Heb. 8).

2. Do a *paragraph summary outline* of one or more of these key New Testament passages: Romans 3 and 4; Romans 6 and 7; Galatians 3—5.

(A *paragraph summary outline* is expressing the

94

teaching of a paragraph in a single sentence. Use a Bible which divides the text into paragraphs; then use your own words to express its content.)

AN OPEN DOOR

THE EVENTS RECORDED IN Exodus through
Deuteronomy report Israel's redemption from
Egypt—and give us a picture of our own redemption from sin. In the early chapters of this book
we've seen several key truths.

We have a deep need for redemption. As Israel was in
slavery, so are all men lost and powerless under the
sway of sin.

Only God's action can provide deliverance. God Himself had to intervene in acts of power to break the
authority of Pharaoh over Israel. God Himself had
to intervene, in Jesus Christ, to free us.

Our new life emerges from death; the Lamb must die.
The Passover lamb's blood on the door protected
Israel from the death angel. It is the blood of
Christ, shed for the sins of the world, which
guarantees our salvation.

*Our new life is to be marked by a holiness which we do
not have.* Israel's response to God after deliverance

demonstrated her need for standards and for a clear revelation of God's expectations. God is concerned about our righteousness as well: We are called to bear the image of His Son. The standard revealed in words in the Law has been revealed in person by Jesus.

We fall short of the goal to which God calls us. The Law defined the pathway of love for Israel, and at the same time demonstrated that Israel constantly fell short. The New Testament also defines, in terms of principles rather than behavior (of grace, rather than the Law), the pathway of love. A look into the New Testament shows us that we, too, fall short of being all that God calls us to be.

These are central messages God gave Israel in the events we've read about. Today the record of the events speaks the same messages to you and me. The last of these messages—the revelation that even after redemption we are in need—launches us into an exciting segment of Scripture. God reminds us that we are a needy people. And with the reminder, He gives us an insight into the way He plans to meet that very need.

THE DAYS AFTER

Often a person who becomes a Christian experiences a special and excited glow. Somehow his life seems different. Somehow he seems different himself.

For some this glow persists for days or weeks. But sooner or later, life brings a sudden jolt. The love we felt for others in the first flush of realizing God's love for us fades, and we're irritated by that clod of a co-worker. We get angry at someone close to us—a parent or child or brother.

Sometimes the alcoholic feels suddenly free from dependence on drink . . . until the urge returns with overwhelming intensity as he passes a familiar bar.

We think that salvation has freed us from temptation—and then we find our thought returning to old paths, and old desires returning with a nagging urgency.

We discover after our conversion a sudden enjoyment in prayer, and a real interest in the Bible. Then . . . after a time, we no longer want to pray. And the Bible once again becomes dull and dry and meaningless.

Often when such a relapse happens the new believer is confused. Sometimes he wonders if he has lost the salvation he had. Sometimes he questions the reality of the conversion experience. Very often a person blames himself, feeling deeply the shame of falling into old patterns of life after being so sure that the old was gone once and for all.

It's very helpful, when we're captured by such feelings, to learn the lesson that God taught Israel in the events that followed the giving of the Law. Israel had experienced redemption. But Israel had a continued and continual need for God. Only the divine provision could lift individuals and the nation beyond themselves, to become the person and the people God redeemed them to be.

A PICTURE OF REALITY

Exodus 25–27

God knows the need of believers for continual cleansing and enablement. Israel had not yet seen herself as a still-needy people. Yet God began to meet the need before it was understood. His provision was in the Tabernacle—a tent of worship which became the only place where Israelites might approach God. (Later it was replaced by a single Temple, erected in the Promised Land.)

Looking back, the writer of the New Testament Book of Hebrews focuses on Exodus 25:9. The Tabernacle was to be made "according to all that I show you concerning the pattern of the tabernacle, and of all its furniture." The New Testament points to this as evidence that the Tabernacle is a kind of mirror of reality. Its design reflects truth about our relationship with God and the special provision God has made for us. In the New Testament the Tabernacle is called "a copy and shadow of what is in heaven" (Heb. 8:5). Looking at it, we can discover much about the reality you and I are experiencing in Christ.

Exodus 32–34

While Moses was receiving instructions on the construction of the Tabernacle, an event was taking place at the base of the mountain which clearly revealed Israel's need for it. Moses had been on the mount receiving instruction from God. All through this time thunderings and flashing lightning gave constant testimony to the presence of God. Yet as the days passed and Moses did not return, Israel became restive. A number of the people went to Aaron, Moses' brother, and insisted that he make an idol. He took their gold, and melted it to shape a golden calf, and proclaimed a "feast to the Lord." The molten calf was presented to the people with the announcement, "These are your gods, O Israel, who brought you up out of the land of Egypt" (32:4).

When Moses returned, those who had sinned were severely judged. Yet even those who had not actually been involved bore their share of the responsibility. How could God identify Himself with a sinning people?

Yet it was just this, the presence of God, that made Israel distinct. As Moses prayed, "Is it not in thy going with us, so that we are distinct, I and thy people, from all other people on the face of the earth?" (Ex. 33:16). God's presence distinguished His people from all others.

In God's presence there must be found a remedy for the constant outbreaks of sin which threatened Israel—and which threaten you and me today.

Exodus 35–40

The failure of Israel at Sinai demonstrated graphically that even a redeemed people constantly need God. The failure of the people prepared them to sense that need and to see the importance of the Tabernacle. In each detail, the Tabernacle spoke of God's provision for His people. In each detail the people could discover another dimension of what God's presence with them would mean.

These chapters seem to be a mere repetition of what has already been said in Exodus 25—27. But they are more than that. They illustrate for us the fact that the provision God has planned must be appropriated by His people. We must build into the fabric of our lives all that God says He has readied for us.

TABERNACLE

In a very vital way the Tabernacle is a "type" (an Old Testament character, event, or institution which has a place and purpose in Bible history but which also, by divine design, foreshadows something future). In every aspect the Tabernacle pictures the relationship between God and a redeemed people. In every aspect the Tabernacle shows us how God's presence with us not only sets us apart from all others, but meets our need for daily deliverance from sin's power.

What, then, was the Tabernacle like—and what does it tell us about our own need to experience freedom?

The Tabernacle plan. The Tabernacle was a large tent, surrounded by an outer court—a long, rectangular enclosure 150 by 75 feet. It was portable, the walls of the court and the tent itself being made of curtains. The Tabernacle was a sanctuary, a dwelling place for God. It consisted of an outer "Holy Place" and an inner "Holy of Holies" into

FIGURE V

THE COURT AND TABERNACLE

which the high priest alone could enter, and then only once a year.

During the time in the wilderness, God's presence was a visible thing, marked by a cloudy fiery pillar which always stood over the Tabernacle. When erected, the Tabernacle stood in the middle of the camp, with the people ranged around it on every side.

God chooses to dwell in the center of His people. He is to be the center of our lives. Never just on the periphery.

The Tabernacle furnishings. It is, however, in the furnishings of the Tabernacle that we gain insight into what God's presence in our lives provides. Each of the furnishings speaks clearly of a ministry of God through which the believer is protected from himself and enabled to become all that God intends.

(1) *The bronze altar.* There was only one door to this "Tent of Meeting." Any person who wanted to come into God's presence had to come through the

one door which the plan of God provided. At the door, placed so that no one who entered could avoid it, stood the bronze altar. This was the altar of sacrifice: the place on which daily the prescribed offerings for Israel would be laid. As Leviticus would later make clear, "the life of the flesh is in the blood; and I have given it for you upon the altar to make atonement for your souls; for it is the blood that makes atonement" (Lev. 17:11). No one could approach God or receive the benefits of His presence without entering by the door of sacrifice and atonement.

Later Jesus would use this same picture in speaking of Himself. "I am the gate," He announced. "Whoever enters through me will be saved. I am the good shepherd. The good shepherd lays down his life for the sheep" (Jn. 10:9, 11). The message is clear. Access to the benefits God has provided for us is ours only as we come to God in the single way He has planned.

(2) *The bronze laver.* The laver, a large container for water, was made of the same bronze metal as the altar. It stood at the entrance of the Tabernacle itself, and was for the cleansing of those who entered the Presence. Jesus used a similar symbolism at the time of the Last Supper when He washed the disciples' feet. They have been cleansed, He tells them, so they do not need another "bath." But as they have walked on the dusty roads after the bathing, their feet need to be washed again and again (cf. Jn. 13:2-12).

Believers have been cleansed by the blood of

FIGURE VI

THE TABERNACLE AND ITS FURNITURE

Christ. Yet daily we need to turn to God for cleansing, relying on that single sacrifice as the source of daily cleansing. For the apostle John this provision is clearly ours: "If we confess our sins [those daily failures that mar the lives even of those who experienced salvation], he is faithful and just and will forgive us our sins and purify us from all unrighteousness" (I Jn. 1:9).

The continual cleansing each of us needs is provided in Christ, and pictured in the laver before the Tabernacle entrance. Purified, we can freely enter the presence of our God.

(3) *The table of shewbread.* Immediately inside the first veil a table was set. On this table, placed to the right in the chamber, was kept a constant supply of fresh food and drink. All that the believer needs to strengthen and supply him is found in God's presence.

(4) *The golden candlestick.* To the left as one entered the first chamber stood a seven-branched candlestick, so designed that there was a constant flow of oil to feed it. This was the sole source of light in the Tabernacle. Natural light was blocked off by a series of curtains and coverings.

In the presence of God, He alone provides the light we need to see our way. And that light is enough.

(5) *Golden altar of incense.* Centered before the veil that separated the Holy Place and the Holy of Holies stood an altar of incense. This altar spoke of worship and of other dimensions of prayer (cf. Rev. 8:3, 4). Here praise and prayer blended as the

priests approached the presence of God, awed and yet exalted by His closeness.

(6) *The Ark of the Covenant.* There was a single article of furniture within the Holy of Holies. The thick veil that separated this chamber was moved only once a year, when the high priest entered there alone on the high and holy Day of Atonement, carrying the blood of sacrifice to sprinkle on the Mercy Seat. It was here, in the inner chamber, that the presence of God was focused.

The veil itself communicated a message. The New Testament clarifies it. "The Holy Spirit was showing by this that the way into the Most Holy Place had not yet been disclosed as long as the first tabernacle was still standing" (Heb. 9:8). The Bible tells us that at the moment of Christ's death, "the curtain of the temple was torn in two from top to bottom" (Mt. 27:51).

There is for us the fullness of God's presence, a fullness that goes beyond even the rich provision God made for His Old Testament people.

What then was the ark, and what did it speak of? The ark itself was a gold-covered chest, containing special reminders of God's work for His people. There was a container of manna, speaking of complete and miraculous provision. There were the tablets on which the Ten Commandments were written, speaking of the righteousness God alone can produce. Later there was Aaron's rod, which had miraculously budded and borne fruit, speaking of God's power to bring life from the dead. The ark itself was named "of the covenant," a reminder of God's commitment to fulfill His promises.

On the ark rested a special cover, overlaid with gold, and called the "Mercy Seat." Here, between two carved angels whose wings met over the center of the Mercy Seat, the blood of the annual sin offering for the people of Israel was sprinkled. Here was the very focus of God's meeting with man. At the Mercy Seat, God invested the fullness of His own presence . . . and it was here alone that God fully touched men.

This is why the act of God in tearing the veil from top to bottom is so significant. In that act which accompanied the Crucifixion we are told that there is no longer a curtain between the believer and the full experience of God's presence. No wonder Hebrews invites, "Let us then approach the throne of grace with confidence, so that we may receive mercy and find grace to help us in our time of need" (Heb. 4:16). For the believer today, who has come through the one door to God, and entered, cleansed, into a relationship with the Lord in which God strengthens him, guides him, and invites him to worship, there is even more. There is full and complete welcome into the holiest place of all—the very presence of God where miracles are the norm, and where righteousness is worked in the personality of men who have passed from death into life.

FOR US

It is doubtful if Israel understood all that the Tabernacle and its furnishings promised. Only in the light of God's full revelation in Christ do we understand.

But while the Tabernacle pictures for us realities we are able now to experience in Christ, the Tabernacle also spoke a great message to Israel.

Israel had sinned and failed to meet the standard God's holiness imposed. Conscious of her failure, the people of God must have finally crouched in shame, wondering how they could ever be restored again to relationship with their God. And wondering too how they could ever find strength to live as a people whose holiness must approach His.

At this point in time, when the people stripped themselves of their ornaments in mourning (Ex. 33:6), God had His remedy ready. Again the commandments were repeated (Ex. 34), and then all Israel was invited to bring their offerings, to construct a Tabernacle in which God might dwell.

The presence of God within Israel's camp, and the promise that presence carried—reflected in every aspect of the Tabernacle and its furnishings—were the divine answer to man's need. A redeemed Israel would continue to be in daily need of God. And their God would be there . . . available and able.

This is, of course, the great message of God to us today. We too continually need God. In our own strength we fail. That first moment of salvation is the beginning of a process of transformation—it is *not* the completion of God's work. For our daily need there is only one answer: God's presence within us. He alone can meet every need.

GOING DEEPER

to personalize

1. What has your own life been like since you became a Christian? Draw a line in the box below that visualizes your own experience. It can be uphill, downhill, or up and down. But try to have it reflect what has happened *after* you came to know Christ.

2. Jot down several of the needs you have discovered in yourself since becoming a Christian. (For instance, pp. 97. and 98 talk about several common needs—from strength to resist temptation to assurance of forgiveness, etc.).

3. Look through the furnishings of the Tabernacle and see if any of them speak to the needs you listed. What do you think God is saying to *you* through this Old Testament institution?

4. To get a feel for this section of Scripture, read Exodus 35—40, and underline any verses or sections which seem particularly significant to you.

to probe

1. Pages 97 and 98 of this chapter define five messages which have been delivered by God in the Book of Exodus. Look at each one, and then find at

least two New Testament references which teach the same truth.

2. Read through the text again, and develop a chart showing all the parallels you can find between Israel's experience with the Tabernacle and our own experience.

3. Select one article of furniture of the Tabernacle and write a five-page paper on the reality it foreshadows for the believer.

4. Write a paper on "the contribution of Hebrews 9 to our understanding of the Tabernacle."

IN FELLOWSHIP

THE BOOK OF LEVITICUS is often viewed as God's instructions to Israel on holy living. Before God had spoken from the distance of the mountaintop. Now, with the Tabernacle erected as a place of meeting, God's presence was established among Israel. They were brought into a unique fellowship with God. It was God's "going with" His people that made them distinct from all others (Ex. 33:16).

But how do we live in fellowship with God? If we are to be in relationship with Him, we will need continual cleansing (that being provided in the Tabernacle)—and we will need to express in our daily lives a quality which can be traced to God's presence. The New Testament puts it like this: "Walk in the light, as he is in the light" (I Jn. 1:7).

J. Sidlow Baxter *(Explore the Book,* Vol. I), noting the duel need of continual cleansing and a distinctive life for those in fellowship with God, divides the Book of Leviticus into two parts.

I. The Ground of Fellowship—Sacrifice (1—18)
  A. The Offerings—absolution (1—7)
  B. The Priesthood—mediation (8—10)
  C. The People—purification (11—16)
  D. The Altar—reconciliation (17)
II. The Walk of Fellowship—Separation (18—27)
  A. Regulations concerning the people (18—20)
  B. Regulations concerning the priests (21—22)
  C. Regulations concerning feasts, etc. (23—24)
  D. Regulations concerning Canaan (25—27)

Whether we follow this particular division of the book or not, it is clear on all counts that Leviticus goes into detail about the life-style of the people of God.

Here, detailed explanation of the various offerings and sacrifices is provided (chs. 1—7). Instructions about the priest's consecration and ministries are given (chs. 8—10, 13—17, 21, 22). In addition there is a variety of special instructions, some of which relate to high moral commitment to others (cf. chs. 19, 25), while some seem simply designed to teach them "to make a distinction between the unclean and the clean" (11:47). In the same spirit, the priest is charged: "You are to distinguish between the holy and the common, and between the unclean and the clean" (10:10). God's people were to be constantly sensitive to their position as a people set apart to Him.

Some have gone to great lengths to invent "logical" reasons for some of the commands God gives here. The proscription against pork has, even to this day, led to the imaginative notion that pork is somehow bad meat. Just a month ago I talked with someone who argued that a pig's digestive system is incomplete, and that consequently waste materials are stored in the body rather than eliminated as by other animals. Thus pork is supposed to be intrinsically dirty—and thus God is justified in His proscribing pork in Israel. (It is a little harder to similarly explain other dietary laws—such as "you shall not boil a kid in its mother's milk.") Yet, later, to teach Peter that the Old Testament economy was passing and that Jew and Gentile were no longer to be viewed as distinct, God caused a great sheet to be lowered and commanded Peter to "Kill and eat." Peter objected. These were unclean animals. And the word of God came. "Do not call anything impure that God has made clean" (Acts 10:9-15).

Later Paul would write in Romans, "I am fully convinced that no food is unclean in itself. But if anyone regards something as unclean, then for him it is unclean" (Rom. 14:14, 15).

The point is simply this. Some things are immoral and thus unclean in themselves. Adultery, for instance, is never right. Such things are rooted in the very nature of man as God has created him, and in God's own character and righteousness. But many things we read of here in Leviticus do not

115

have intrinsic rightness and wrongness. They were unclean because God said they were to be so regarded by His people.

Why did God create a whole set of unclean things? In answering, we do not need to give a logical excuse for each item, as some attempt with the dietary laws. Instead, we need to realize that God was acting to train and discipline His people. He was working with them to give them a sense of their own identity as His people, and to help them realize constantly the privilege—and responsibility—of fellowship with Him.

In the closing chapters of Leviticus God exhorts Israel to walk in His statutes and observe His commandments. He says, "And I will walk among you, and will be your God, and you will be my people" (Lev. 26:12). With this encouragement God also gave a warning. If the people would not hear, God would bring judgment, and seek by discipline to turn Israel to Him again.

There was a tremendous danger that this people would forget their God. Sinai had demonstrated how quickly and easily they forgot! But now the very pattern of life Israel was invited to in Leviticus made it almost impossible to forget Him. Each meal served as a reminder. The specialness of the offerings and the annual feasts served as reminders. The Sabbath day and its observance gave a weekly reminder. The customs of Israel were designed to constantly remind them that they had a special relationship with God, and were called to walk in fellowship with Him.

116

Many of these customs of Israel are irrelevant to us today. Others have deep typical significance, and speak of Christ. Still others reflect God's own character, and are rooted in the nature of righteousness. But all of them serve as unique reminders to us today of our distinctive relationship with God. We too are a people in fellowship with the Father. We are called to be set apart to Him. In our unique relationship the externals have been largely set aside. Yet in our hearts, attitudes, and responsiveness to God and our fellowmen, we are to be distinctively His. John sums it up for us. "Obedience is the test of whether we really live 'in God' or not. The life of a man who professes to be living in God must bear the stamp of Christ" (I Jn. 2:5, 6, Phillips).

THE PRIESTHOOD

Leviticus does more than summarize the life-style of a people who have been set apart for fellowship with God. It also gives us insight into an Old Testament institution which we need to understand: the priesthood.

There are three reasons why we need to give special attention to the priesthood.

1. It is a basic Old Testament institution. We cannot really understand the Old Testament without some grasp of its nature and function.

2. Christ is called our High Priest. We gain an understanding of His ministry to us when we study the priesthood.

3. Believers today are "being built into a spiritual house to be a holy priesthood, offering spiritual sacrifices acceptable to God through Jesus Christ" (I Pet. 2:5). Since we are "a chosen people, a royal priesthood" (2:9), we need to see the meaning of priesthood if we're to understand our own calling as Christians.

We hear very little of priesthood today. The whole priestly system is foreign to Protestantism, and to our culture. But if we are to learn how to live as ministers of the New Covenant (II Cor. 3:6), and break out of the tragically passive role of laymen, we need to rediscover our identity as believer-priests—every one called to minister for and before his God.

Mediators. We need to begin our survey of the priesthood by noting that the priest served as a mediator between God and man. Hebrews 5 says it: the priest is "selected from among men and is appointed to represent them in matters related to God, to offer gifts and sacrifices for sins" (5:1).

The individual in Israel who wished to approach God brought his offering to the priest. That offering may have been an offering of obligation (one which had to be made because of guilt for sin), or a freewill offering of thanks or praise. But either kind of offering must be brought to God through a priest. The priest, who served the altar, was the doorkeeper. His ministry kept the approach to God open.

At the same time, the priest taught and interpreted God's revelation. "You are to distinguish between the holy and the common, between the unclean and the clean," Aaron and his sons were told. "And you are to teach the people of Israel all the statutes which the Lord has spoken to them by Moses" (Lev. 10:10, 11).

Thus the mediating priest was not only a person through whom an individual might approach God—he was also a person who understood and interpreted God's words to the people. Communication between God and man in early Israel was focused in the person of the priest.[5]

Aaron and his descendants were set aside for this door-keeping ministry. In the land the priests and the Levites (the other descendants of Levi) were not given territory as were the other families of Israel. They were instead dedicated to care for the things of God. Special cities were set aside for them to live in throughout the territories of the other tribes. But there was no land they were to call their own. Instead God was to be their portion, and they were supported by an offering of a tenth of all that was produced by the other tribes. Their ministry was so important it required total dedication.

What, then, does the Old Testament tell us about this class of mediators whose ministry foreshadows both the work of Christ—and our own?

Exodus 28–29. With the Tabernacle pattern revealed, God instructed Moses to set Aaron and his sons aside from the people of Israel to serve Him as priests. They, and especially Aaron the high priest,

[5]Later the prophet was introduced into Israel. We will look at the prophetic ministry in another study.

were given holy garments "for glory and for beauty" (28:2). One striking feature: the names of the 12 tribes was engraved on onyx stones and attached to the shoulder clasps of Aaron's garment, and on the breastplate. Thus Aaron was to "bear the names of the sons of Israel in the breastpiece of judgment upon his heart, when he goes into the holy place, to bring them to continual remembrance before the Lord" (28:29).

In the breast piece too were the Urim and Thummin, which some believe were three polished stones, on which "yes," "no," and nothing were engraved. When Israel sought to know God's will, God guided the hand of the priest to select His answer as he reached blindly inside the breast piece pocket. Thus the "judgment of the people of Israel" was also borne "upon his heart before the Lord continually" (Ex. 28:30). The priest carried the people by name before the Lord, and God's will was carried on his heart back to them.

The Exodus passage also speaks of the priests' ordination, and points out that, for Aaron and his sons, sacrifice must be made. All associated with their ministry was set aside for service by the sprinkling of sacrificial blood. To maintain that blood-won point of contact with God, a "continual burnt offering" was offered daily "at the door of the tent of meeting before the Lord, where," God says, "I will meet with you, to speak there to you. There I will meet with the people of Israel, and it shall be sanctified by my glory" (29:42, 43).

Leviticus 10. Following the ordination of the

120

priests (reported in Lev. 8, 9) an incident occurred which emphasized the critical role the priest was to play. Nadab and Abihu, two of Aaron's sons, broke the ordained pattern of ministry, and "offered unholy fire" before the Lord (10:1). God acted immediately: the pair died there before the Lord.

Verses 8—10 of this chapter help explain. No priest was to drink alcoholic beverages when ministering: a priest must be fully aware. The priest was called to "distinguish between the holy and common" and "to teach the people of Israel all the statutes" which the Lord had spoken. One who taught holiness must be holy.

Leviticus 13, 14. The ministry of the priest in evaluating and judging is seen in a task assigned here. The priest was to examine diseased individuals and places. Leprosy, a disease that separated the sick person from society as unclean, was diagnosed by the priest on the basis of clear instructions in Scripture.

When the person recovered, the priest also was to examine him and pronounce him cleansed, and officially restore him to fellowship.

The priest did not cure. But the priest did make a distinction between clean and unclean, sick and healed.

Leviticus 21, 22. This passage emphasizes the holiness of the priests. "They shall be holy to their God . . .," says 21:6, "for they offer the offerings by fire to the Lord." Thus the priest was under special restrictions as far as marriage was concerned. No one of the Aaronic family could fulfill the priestly function when ceremonially unclean. Baxter comments on this:

> *All* the sons of Aaron, whether young or old, defective or normal, were priests to Jehovah, by virtue of their birth and life-relationship with Aaron; and nothing could break that relationship. Yet those among them who were physically defective were not allowed to officiate at the altar or enter within the veil of the sanctuary (xxi. 21-23). And those who were in any way defiled were not allowed even to eat of the priests' portion (xxii. 6-7). Even so, every true believer is a priest by virtue of life-giving union with the Lord Jesus, and nothing can break that union. But all Christians do not enjoy the same intimacy of fellowship, or exercise the same ministry within the veil! Union is one thing; communion is another.[6]

CHRIST'S HIGH PRIESTHOOD

Hebrews 4:14–10:25

This extended section of the New Testament discusses the high priesthood of Jesus. It compares Him to the Aaronic priesthood of the Old Testament, and contrasts His ministry to theirs.

Chapters four and five of Hebrews emphasize the necessity for the priest to be identified with

---

[6]J. Sidlow Baxter, *Explore the Book*, Vol. I (Grand Rapids: Zondervan), p. 135.

those he serves. A mediator must have contact with those who need his ministry.

Hebrews 7 emphasizes the primacy of Christ's priesthood, stressing its superiority over the Aaronic. The passage also points out a crucial concept: perfection could not come through the old priesthood. By a continual and repetitive ministry the Aaronic priests held the door to God open. But only a permanent priest could save completely, and guarantee our access. As believers, we no longer need a human priest to meet us at the door, and then to turn within while we stand outside and wait. Christ, in His death and resurrection, has thrown the door wide open, and invited us to enter. Christ Himself, living forever, is God's eternal guarantee that the door to eternal life shall never be closed to us.

Chapter 8 of Hebrews elaborates on this. Christ is priest of an entirely new system, a system which reaches within men's hearts to transform them. According to Hebrews 9 this required that Christ as High Priest present a perfect offering—one able to clear the conscience of the worshiper. Chapter 10 goes on to develop the efficacy of Christ's sacrifice. Through His sacrifice we have been made holy once for all. We are now able to enter confidently into the very presence of God. "Let us then," says Hebrews in introducing the priesthood theme, "approach the throne of grace with confidence, so that we may receive mercy and find grace to help us in our time of need" (4:16). Our ever-living High Priest, who has made a single sacrifice to perfect us, has thrown wide open the door at which the Old Testament priest once stood—and commanded us to enter boldly.

OUR PRIESTHOOD

This brief survey of some of the aspects of priesthood helps us to understand our present standing with God. Because of Christ, the old need of a doorkeeper is gone.

But what then about *our* priesthood? How are we to serve?

In part, we serve in worship. The offerings made on the altar were not all for sin. Many were offerings of thanksgiving and praise, expressing the joy of communion with the Lord. Revelation speaks of the prayers of the saints, rising up to God as a pleasing incense.

In part, too, we serve our brothers. As Aaron bore the names of Israel before the Lord, and as Jesus bears our names on His heart, so are we to carry the names and needs of our brothers before the Lord. There are fellow priests of ours who experience need. There are some too who are temporarily unclean. They have a relationship with God, but are not experiencing communion. These too we serve—not only bringing them to God in prayer, but also reaching out to them, to teach, to encourage, to discipline, to care.

And there is another class of people. These have never met Christ or come to know Him in a saving way. The concept of priesthood is very important here in helping us understand ourselves. The priest was chosen "from among men." He established a point of contact with them based on his likeness to them. The New Testament stresses the fact that Jesus too became fully human, that He might be able to "sympathize with our weaknesses" (Heb. 4:15). He never sinned; yet He knew fully all that it means to be a person and subject to human weakness.

Because of his identification with humanity, the priest was able to reach out to grasp the hand of the sinner and lead him to God. Our priestly ministry carries that same demand, the demand that we reach out to people, confessing our common identity. By linking ourselves with them in common need, we can draw them to God.

GOING DEEPER

to personalize

1. Select at least three of the following sections of Leviticus to read. Select on the basis of your own interests; read quickly but carefully to get the flavor of this book.

> (1) *Leviticus 6, 7.* In these chapters you'll read about the sacrifices at which priests officiated.
>
> (2) *Leviticus 11.* This reports the dietary laws which were part of the life-style of Israel and reminded them of their specialness.
>
> (3) *Leviticus 15.* This describes causes of cere-

monial uncleanness. These were things
which disqualified people temporarily
from contact with God at the Tabernacle,
yet were not rooted in moral misbehavior.

(4) *Leviticus 19*. This passage repeats a number
of the case law demonstrations of love. It
contains the key thought, "You shall love
your neighbor as yourself: I am the Lord."

(5) *Leviticus 21*. The special obligation of holiness is explained here.

(6) *Leviticus 23*. Here the festivals of Israel are
described again.

(7) *Leviticus 25*. The "year of Jubilee" was a
unique feature of Israel's way of life, demonstrating an unmatched sense of responsibility for others. Read this to get a deep
insight into the heart of God . . . and God's
desire for our own attitude toward others.

(8) *Leviticus 26*. The results of Israel's choice to
adopt or reject the holy life-style God has
commanded are described here. This
chapter gives a striking preview of the actual history of Israel.

2. Read the chapters in the Old Testament relating to priesthood, and jot down notes on everything which you believe has some application to
your own role as a believer-priest.

3. Read through Hebrews 4:14—10:25 quickly,
jotting down anything which helps you understand
what a priest is and does—and how Jesus' ministry
as High Priest relates to you.

to probe

1. Write a paper on the offerings (Lev. 1—7), defining how they help us understand our own priestly ministry. (Note that three of these offerings were voluntary, two required.)

2. Examine several books on Christology (the person and work of Jesus). Look particularly for what the book says about Jesus' present ministry for believers, and how this is related to His priesthood. Look in a number of sources: this theme is not developed by many. Report on your discoveries in a paper of several pages.

9

Numbers 1–20

THE CHOICE

LAURA'S FACE CONTORTED AS she stood sobbing in my office. Laura was a teenager whose home was a tragedy. She had just become a Christian, and it was so hard for her. She was fighting against the pull of her past and the difficulties of her present, and she was feeling deep frustration and guilt and pain.

It was good to talk with Laura. For her sense of guilt, it was good to remind her that God has forgiven her, and so she can forgive herself too. For her frustration, it was good to point out that everyone makes mistakes. We all do the "dumb" kind of things that were frustrating her . . . and we're all allowed to. It's part of growing, and the exciting thing is that God promises we *will* grow in Him . . . grow beyond ourselves and our inadequacies toward Christ's likeness.

For the pain of her present there was a different

kind of message. She didn't need sympathy or pity, but instead only needed help to face the problems her circumstances created. In the face of her difficulties, all that our family could promise was to help her be responsible.

RESPONSIBLE

This was just the issue facing Israel at the beginning of the Book of Numbers. They had been redeemed from slavery by God's power. They had been taught His will, and given a Law that revealed His character. Provision had been made to cleanse the sins that would inevitably come and the doorway to God and His forgiveness had been guaranteed through Tabernacle, sacrifice, and priesthood. The forgiven people had been instructed how to live in fellowship with their Lord.

And now came a new message. "Since you have been provided with everything you need in order to live a holy life, you are responsible." Israel was to face difficult and challenging circumstances. But there were no acceptable excuses for failing to respond to God. In each situation Israel was now responsible for its choices—and responsible too for the outcome. Israel's experience would inevitably be a direct consequence of its decision to follow—or to reject—the leading of God.

Laura was young, as a person and as a Christian. Learning to be responsible was a hard lesson. But it's hard for us at any age. Some of us learn the lesson of responsibility only after a great deal of pain, as wrong choices work out their results in our lives. Some of us learn quickly, from others.

God has included a catalog of events in Numbers 1—20 just so that we *can* learn the lesson of responsibility from Israel—and not have to learn it the hard way. "These things happened to them as examples and were written down as warnings for us," I Corinthians 10:11 tells us. "So, if you think you are standing firm, be careful that you don't fall!" It is comforting to understand our position in Christ as forgiven people. But it is important to realize that however exalted our position, as we live our daily lives we must accept responsibility for our choices and act as redeemed people—lest we fall.

Numbers 1–10. Here is where we see the first indication that the great mob of people who swarmed

FIGURE VII

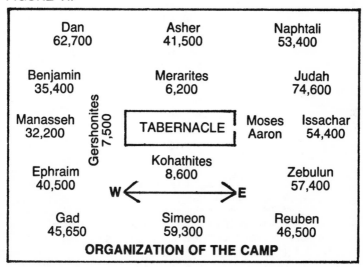

ORGANIZATION OF THE CAMP

out of Egypt are not to be treated as a responsible nation. A census was taken, with the men of military age numbering 603,550. (This figure is given in several different texts, though in some it is rounded off: Ex. 12:37; 38:26; Num. 1:46; 2:32; 11:21. The later census of 26:41 shows similarity but significant change over a 38-year period.) The total population probably ranged somewhere between two and two and a half million persons.

Tribal marching and camping positions were set, duties of the Levites defined, and a system of

FIGURE VIII

ISRAEL MARCHING
Judah

Issachar

Zebulun

Gershon and Merari*

Reuben

Simeon

Gad

Kohath*

Ephraim

Manasseh

Benjamin

Dan

Asher

Naphtali

*The Levites were divided into two companies (see Num. 10:14-27). The sons of Gershon and Merari carried the Tabernacle itself, while the Kohathites carried the holy articles from the Tabernacle. With the order of march arranged as it was, the carriers of the Tabernacle had time to set it up before the holy things arrived.

---

trumpet calls set to signal assembly, order of departure, alarms, etc.

As the people of Israel marched they were to respond to the direct leading of God. The pillar of cloud and fire which had appeared as Israel left Egypt (Ex. 13:21) now rested over the Tabernacle. When the cloud rested, the people remained in camp. But when in the morning the cloud lifted up, they set out, and followed the cloud as God led them where He chose. As the Bible says, "At the command of the Lord they encamped, and at the command of the Lord they set out; they kept the charge of the Lord, at the command of the Lord by Moses" (Num. 9:23). Even in this, the people were being taught to respond to God. God's people must always look to Him for guidance, and go, or wait, at His command.

THREE LESSONS

Numbers 11:1–12:15

When Israel moved away from Sinai after having been camped there some eleven months, three incidents occurred which were truly "examples" for Israel (I Cor. 10:11). Each involved a rejection of God, and each was an immediate occasion for judgment. Israel was being taught the difficult lesson of responsibility. As God's people, they were to respond to Him with trust and obedience. If they failed to respond, they had to accept the tragic consequences.

Numbers 11:1-3: rejection of God's guidance. It took only three days of journeying in desert country for the Israelites to revert to a pattern they had established before they arrived at Sinai. Forgetting all that God had done for them, they let discomfort dominate their thinking. They "complained in the hearing of the Lord about their misfortunes" (11:1). This was an explicit rejection of God as the One who guided them and had guided them from the beginning. They ignored the supernatural provision of the fiery, cloudy pillar that directed every move.

God immediately acted in judgment. Fire destroyed some outlying parts of the camp. In panic the people turned to Moses, who prayed, and the fire was controlled.

Numbers 11:4-35: rejection of God's provision. Shortly afterward the people began to complain about something else. They became dissatisfied with their diet, and were ready to trade their freedom for the meat and vegetables they had enjoyed in Egypt. The manna which God provided was despised, and "every man at the door of his tent" complained and plotted because of a craving for meat.

This rejection of God's provision was a last straw to Moses, who had long felt the burden of leading a people who behaved like a squalling infant (11:12). God responded to Moses' need by distributing his leadership responsibility and gift to seventy of the elders. And He responded to the people. God had Moses tell the people that the next day they would have meat. Meat enough for a whole month, "until it comes out at your nostrils and becomes loathsome to you" (11:20). "You have rejected the Lord who is among you" (v. 20), is the divine commentary on their behavior and its meaning.

God provided meat by bringing a great flock of quail (perhaps like the giant flocks of carrier pigeons which in the early days of our continent darkened the sky for days). The quail flew about three feet off the ground (vs. 31), and for two days were gathered by the bushel. Meat for the millions had been provided.

But when the people began to eat, a great plague struck the camp. Thousands and thousands of the murmurers died (vss. 33, 34). The people who had rejected God and His provision bore the dreadful consequences of their choice.

Numbers 12: rejection of God's appointed. Shortly afterward another incident of rebellion occurred. This time Miriam and Aaron, Moses' sister and brother, resented the special role Moses was given by God. They were aware that God had used them as well as Moses. So they challenged Moses' authority.

God responded by angrily pointing out the special relationship He had chosen to have with Moses; "he is entrusted with all my house [hold]" (vs. 7). In judgment Miriam was stricken with leprosy, and put out of the camp for seven days. Afterward she was healed in answer to Moses' prayer. (Aaron, who served as high priest, would have been disqualified from his office if he had been similarly judged.)

The entire nation was to learn by this experience: everyone waited for those seven days, and the people did not set out on their journey until Miriam was brought in again, healed (vs. 15).

Why did God deal so harshly and so decisively with the people at fault in these three incidents? These things "happened to them as examples." Israel was about to make a vitally important decision—one that would affect their future drastically. On the journey to the place of decision, God permitted these three incidents that Israel might learn the lesson of responsibility. Notice the parallel in the incidents in each situation:

■ Circumstances, rather than God's presence, were given priority.
■ God's clearly revealed will and purposes were rejected.
■ The rejecting attitude was expressed in actions.
■ Israel's wrong choices led to judgment and suffering.

In unmistakable and dramatic ways Israel was shown that they were now responsible for their own choices. Whenever they chose to turn away from God, evil results would inevitably follow.

THE CHOICE

Numbers 13, 14

Israel had been given instruction in responsibility

136

on the way to the Promised Land. When they arrived at the borders of Palestine, Moses sent 12 men out in pairs to "spy out the land." They were to evaluate the strength of the peoples, their numbers, "and whether the land is rich or poor" (13:20). God was giving Israel information, that the dangers might be known and weighed against their confidence in God.

Ten of the 12 spies were overawed by the strength of the enemy and the fortified towns they found there. Two of the spies, Caleb and Joshua, encouraged the people to trust God: "Let us go up at once, and occupy it; for we are well able to overcome it" (13:30). But the fears of the others prevailed. Crying in fright and anguish, the whole congregation was ready to choose other leaders to guide them back to Egypt.

Stunned by the choice Israel was making, Moses and Aaron "fell on their faces before all the assembly of the congregation," and Caleb and Joshua tore their clothing (an action indicating depth of feeling) and urged Israel, "Do not rebel against the Lord;. . . their protection is removed from them, and the Lord is with us" (14:9).

This affirmation of faith showed vividly the response that Israel should have made when faced with the choice. Instead "all the congregation said to stone [Caleb and Joshua] with stones."

The choice had been made.

Now, as a responsible people, Israel had to accept the full consequences of its decision.

God's appearance. At this point the Lord visibly

137

intervened. His "glory" suddenly flashed from the Tabernacle. The action of Israel justified their total destruction . . . God could make of Moses alone a greater people than Israel. But Moses again prayed for the people, and they were pardoned. Yet even with the pardon Israel would still bear the consequences of their action. "None of the men who have seen my glory and my signs which I wrought in Egypt and in the wilderness, and yet have put me to the proof these ten times and have not harkened to my voice, shall see the land which I swore to give to their fathers; and none of those who despised me shall see it" (Num. 14:22, 23).

Only Caleb and Joshua were exempted, because they had responded with trust. The rest would be led out again into the wilderness, to wander there for 38 years. "Your dead bodies shall fall in this wilderness; and all of your number numbered from twenty years old and upward, who have murmured against me, not any shall come into the land where I swore I would make you dwell, except Caleb . . . and Joshua" (Num. 14:29, 30).

When their children had learned to accept their responsibility to trust and to obey God, then they would come into the Land of Promise.

A people who would not learn could never know the Promised Land's rest.

Unfair? Lest we think this severe judgment was unfair, we need to look at the aftermath. When Moses told the people the judgment God had determined, they "mourned greatly." And the next morning they jumped up—and mounted an attack

138

on the land they'd been unwilling to approach. But God had commanded them to turn back to the wilderness.

Moses cried out, "Why now are you transgressing the command of the Lord, for that will not succeed?" But they stumbled on up to meet the enemy, though God's Ark and presence remained in the camp. They were defeated and pursued.

The people had demonstrated again that they simply would not listen to God or respond to Him. Over and over their failure to be obedient led them into disaster. Yet they were now responsible. The lesson had to be learned. Until it was learned, the people of Israel would experience tragic consequences with each wrong choice.

THE LOST REST

Hebrews 3:7-11

This New Testament passage is the divine commentary on the event we have just reviewed. It also contains one of the Bible's clearest explanations of the believer's responsibility. Quoting Psalm 95:7-11, the Scripture focuses on the attitude of the Israelites who came out of Egypt. Their hearts were hardened against God, and "always going astray."

The basic lack of trust that characterized these people led them to disobey when they heard the will of God expressed.

Hebrews 4 goes on to apply this incident directly to us today. "Today if you hear his voice," the

Scripture warns, "do not harden your hearts." Because distrust kept Israel from obeying God, the people were unable to enter the land of promise. They never knew rest from their wanderings in the desolation of the wilderness . . . and they died there. How does this apply to us? "There remains, then," says Scripture, "a sabbath-rest for the people of God." There remains an experience with God in which we face life and meet its challenges with peace in our hearts, with confidence that God's good is being worked out in every circumstance. We can miss that experience of peace only by "following their [the Israelites'] example of disobedience."

All this helps us see clearly just what the nature of Christian responsibility is. What responsibility?

FIGURE IX

BELIEVER'S RESPONSIBILITY	
ISRAEL	**US TODAY**
HEAR GOD'S WORD	HEAR GOD'S WORD
ATTITUDE: UNBELIEF	ATTITUDE:
ACTION: DISOBEY	ACTION:
RESULT: WILDERNESS EXPERIENCE ("Not enter His Rest")	RESULT:

Trust God, and express that trust in obedience. As we make Him the focus and goal of our lives, God brings us into the fullness of His rest. The believer's responsibility always remains sure, whether under the Law or under Grace. Redemption's story is one . . . a story replayed at different times on different stages, but with a unifying theme. Redemption brings men and women to God, frees and cleanses them, and provides a choice. Wilderness or promised land. Disobedience or obedience. Unbelief, or a complete and childlike trust in the God who has broken our chains and who promises to accompany our forgiveness with rest. The choice is ours.

THE LOST GENERATION

Numbers 15–20

The generation that stood at the entrance to Canaan had thrown away the Promised Land. How striking that the first words of Numbers 15 are these: "The Lord said to Moses, 'Say to the people of Israel, When you come into the land. . . .'" One generation had lost its opportunity to know rest, but the children would make a different choice. The children would find in their obedience to God the key to the victory their fathers had dismissed so lightly.

The years that followed were years of continuing rebellion. Korah, a Levite, led a rebellion, and on Moses' word the ground opened to swallow up

Korah and all his followers (Num. 16). The congregation challenged this judgment, and a plague struck 14,700 (Num. 16:41-50). The strain of being the link between a holy God and sinful men was fully recognized now by Moses and by Aaron. To Aaron God said—and now the old man understood—"You and your sons and your fathers' house with you shall bear iniquity in connection with the sanctuary" (18:1). Those close to God know a constant tension and struggle with those who draw back from Him and His Word.

The dreary years passed, and the old spirit of complaint continued to mark Israel to the end (Num. 20:2-9). But the end did come. In the 40th year after deliverance from Egypt, in the 38th year of wilderness wanderings, Aaron died and the role of high priest passed to one of his sons. The old generation was dying, soon to pass away in final outbreaks of rebellion and quick judgment. Then a new generation would come.

That generation would accept the responsibility of redemption. And that generation would come to know God's rest.

GOING DEEPER

to personalize

1. Read several sections of Numbers to get the feel of this Bible book. Select from:
   (1) *Numbers 10*. Organized for the march.
   (2) *Numbers 11, 12*. Lessons in being responsible.

(3) *Numbers 13, 14.* The choice at Kadesh.

(4) *Numbers 16–18.* The vindication of Aaron's priesthood.

(5) *Numbers 20.* Moses' sin; Aaron's death.

2. Two New Testament passages deal explicitly with this section of Scripture. Study one of the two, and write at least two pages on how the New Testament commentary helps you understand—and apply—this section of Scripture.

The two passages: I Corinthians 10:1-13; Hebrews 3:7—4:11.

3. Look at the chart on page 140. How would you fill in the blank area to sum up the pattern of *your* life?

How have you experienced the results of "rest" or "wilderness"?

to probe

1. Trace the concept of obedience in the writings of the apostle John. How does what he says correspond with or contrast to the principle as seen here in Numbers?

2. Do a detailed (5 or more pages) commentary on Hebrews 3:7—4:11, drawing on at least four published discussions of this passage as well as your own thoughts.

NO ENCHANTMENT
AGAINST ISRAEL

WITH NUMBERS 21 WE begin a new and positive chapter in the history of redemption. No, God's people are not suddenly perfect. They still fail. But a new generation begins to take over from the old. The generation which mistrusted and disobeyed is dying out. By Numbers 26 we'll read, "There was not a man of those numbered by Moses and Aaron . . . in the wilderness of Sinai. For the Lord had said of them, 'They shall die in the wilderness.' There was not a man left of them, except Caleb the son of Jephunneh and Joshua the son of Nun" (vss. 64, 65).

This new generation began to respond to God's discipline. And made a great discovery. When God's people are in right relationship with Him, they are fully protected.

FOR US

There's a real temptation in looking at these chapters to launch immediately into application. There's so much here that reminds us of our own experience. We can look at the struggle between old and new generations as a mirror of the struggle between our own old sinful nature and the new nature God has given (cf. Rom. 7; Col. 3:1-17). Gradually Israel learned to respond in the new way—and Israel's experience changed. As we learn to respond and live according to what Paul calls the "new man," we too move from the agony of defeat to the joy of victory.

It's exciting too to study the attack on Israel mounted by Balak, king of Moab. He called for a soothsayer of Mesopotamia, Balaam, to come and curse God's people. This spiritual attack failed; Balaam found it impossible to curse God's people. Speaking by God's direction, he was forced to proclaim, "There is no enchantment against Jacob, no divination against Israel" (Num. 23:23). God's presence among His people was full protection against Satan and his powers.

This was a message one of the women in our church needed recently. She had been under especially heavy pressure for several months, and found her old nature breaking out in all sorts of ugly expressions. Looking for an explanation (and an excuse!) she fastened on Satan: "A demon made me do it." How helpful for my wife to be able to sit down with her and work through Scripture, showing her that the believer is a *protected* person. "The one who is in you is greater than the one who is in the world," John assures us (I Jn. 4:4). In this he not only locates the presence of God *within* the believer and the presence of Satan *without*, but he also promises us the balance of power! No wonder James can say, "Resist the devil, and he will flee from you" (4:7). Because we are "in the charge of God's own Son . . . the evil one must keep his distance" (I Jn. 5:18, Phillips).

Before, all the riches inherent in God's presence were only potential for Israel. They did not appropriate the promises by faith. Now in the new generation we begin to see the promises fulfilled. We begin to realize that every promise of God to us will also become part of our daily experience, as we learn to trust Him. In Israel's history God's people were protected by the presence of their God.

We too are invited to rejoice in just this privilege. Christ is in us. We are in the charge of God's own Son. We too are a protected people.

A SINGLE STORY

There is a definite unity to the story of redemption. The experience of God's Old Testament people as a nation parallels our own experience with God as individuals. The redemption they knew is ours as well. Just as the new generation had to anchor their faith in redemption history, we too need to anchor our confidence in an understanding of what God has done for us.

147

This is why it's important to constantly review what we've seen of redemption. It is important to master the messages of this Old Testament section of God's Word—these four books of Moses. Mastering the messages—committing to memory the themes, content, implications, and the Scripture segments related to each—has several benefits.

■ First, we'll be able to think through the critical aspects of our own experience with God as redeemed people.

■ Second, we'll be able to put together a very significant section of Bible content and history, relating each segment to its place in the whole.

■ Third, we'll be able to study any part of these Old Testament books in the context of the whole. Our interpretation and application of Scripture will be sharper and more accurate because we *know* how these four books of the Old Testament are developed. These are benefits worth having. So use the chart on pages 150, 151. Memorize several sections a day, review regularly, and within a week or so you'll have mastered the message—and be able to think through these four books of the Old Testament.

THE TRANSITION

Numbers 21–25

These lessons from the history of Israel were now a firm foundation on which the new generation might base its life with the Lord. Yet there

were still struggles. The old, unbelieving generation was still with them. In these chapters then we
see a struggle: a struggle in which the tendency to
reject God's ways is matched against the tendency
to respond. Sometimes the nation sins, sometimes it
obeys. In the outcome of each course of action, the
new generation is taught the results of sin—and
given a taste of the fruit of obedience.

Numbers 21 shows the uncertainty and the fluc-
tuations. First Israel bravely vows to do battle "if
thou wilt indeed give this people into my hands."
Confidently they go into battle—and win (vss. 1-3).
Yet shortly after that the people became impatient
and returned to their old habit of murmuring
against Moses. In discipline God sent poisonous
snakes among them. Many died. Then the Lord
told Moses to erect an image of a serpent and lift it
high up on a pole. Moses was to announce to all
that anyone bitten could look at the bronze serpent
and live (vss. 4-9). There was no healing power in
the image. Clearly the healing was from God—and
the individual who responded in faith to seek out
the ridiculous remedy *was* healed. Individuals as
well as the nation had power to choose. The new
generation was being taught that they had to take
their destiny in their own hands.

The final incident in the chapter again shows Israel in battle, and again victorious (21:33-35). God's
promise, "Do not fear him; for I have given him
into your hand, and all his people," was now
enough.

Protected from enemies without. (Num. 22–24). As

FIGURE X

UNDERSTANDING REDEMPTION — Exodus through Deuteronomy

Scripture	Events	Message	Key Word(s)	Key verse
Ex. 1-4	Enslaved in Egypt	*Man needs redemption*	Helplessness	Ex. 2:23b
Ex. 5-11	Plagues on Egypt	*God acts to redeem*	Jehovah	
Ex. 12-15	The journey begun	*Redemption comes through death*	Passover/ sacrifice	
Ex. 15-20	Murmurings on the way to Sinai	*Redeemed people are to be holy*	Law/God's character	
Ex. 20-24	Commandment and Case Law given	*Holiness involves love for God and for men*	Law/God's expectations	
Ex. 25-40	Sacrificial, Tabernacle systems instituted	*Redeemed people need cleansing and enablement.*	Tabernacle	
Lev. 1-27	Life-style under Law defined at Sinai	*Redeemed people are to minister in fellowship.*	Priesthood	

Nu. 1-20	Israel leaves Sinai; rebels; into wilderness	*Redeemed people are responsible to obey.*	Discipline
Nu. 21-Deut. 4	A new generation replaces the old	*Redeemed people are under God's protection.*	Protection
Deut. 5-11	Moses teaches the new generation at the border of Palestine	*Redeemed people are loved—and are to be loving*	Love
Deut. 12-26	Restatement of the Law	*Redeemed people must live in a manner pleasing to God.*	Law/holiness
Deut. 27-30	The new generation called to personal commitment	*Redeemed people are to be committed to God.*	Commitment
Deut. 31-34	Joshua's commission; Moses' final blessing and death	*Redeemed people need to be reminded of their redemption.*	Remember

fear of Israel struck the land, the peoples around began to search for weapons. The king of Moab, Balak, overcome at the "horde" which seemed to him to "cover the face of the earth," attempted to call on spiritual resources to defeat Israel. He sent for a man named Balaam, saying, "For I know that he whom you bless is blessed, and he whom you curse is cursed" (22:6).

There is no reason to doubt that Balaam had some spiritual powers. Israel was warned that when they entered the land they had to destroy all those who were spiritualists, possessed by evil spirits, and "necromancers" (cf. Deut. 18:10). Though Balaam clearly used omens, as did pagan seers, in his divinations (cf. 24:1), it is possible that Balaam was a mouthpiece for God to a pagan people. But it is more likely that the roots of his spiritual power were in the demonic rather than the divine. Throughout Scripture Balaam is spoken of as a negative example. His way and his motives are condemned in the New Testament, and his death is recounted in Numbers 31 as a divine judgment.

At any rate, Balak called on Balaam to curse Israel for him, attempting to mount a supernatural attack on a people against whom his natural resources seemed inadequate. But he had made a fatal error. He was ignorant of the spiritual source of Israel's power, rooted in the presence of Jehovah.

God spoke to Balaam and told him not to go with Balak's messengers. Yet Balaam's greed moved him to ask again. This time God permitted him to go, but warned him sternly that he must speak only the words God would give him.

We can picture Balaam's arrival. Balak had been waiting anxiously. Angrily he insists Balaam hurry and curse Israel. Taking Balaam to a range of hills looking down over encamped Israel, the Moabites offered the sacrifices Balaam instructed them to make—and waited. Balaam spoke. But rather than speaking a curse, Balaam was forced by God to pronounce a blessing!

> From the top of the mountains
>   I see him, from the hills I behold him;
> Lo, a people dwelling alone,
>   and not reckoning itself among the nations.
> Who can count the dust of Jacob,
>   or number the fourth part of Israel?
> Let me die the death of the righteous,
>   and let my end be like his!
> *Numbers 23:9, 10*

Three times the sequence is repeated. Balak takes Balaam to a different height, hoping that from a different viewpoint Israel might be cursed. Yet no matter from where the attack is launched, it returns not as a curse but as a blessing on this people God chose and protected. God has dealt with Israel's sin in sacrifice and forgiveness. Thus,

> He has not beheld misfortune in Jacob;
>   nor has he seen trouble in Israel.
> The Lord their God is with them,

and the shout of a king is among them.
God brings them out of Egypt;
  they have as it were the horns of
    the wild ox.
For there is no enchantment against
Jacob,
  no divination against Israel;
  now it shall be said of Jacob and Israel,
  "What has God wrought!"

Numbers 23:21-23

It is God who works in His people. We are His workmanship. Protected by His presence, there is no enchantment against us.

The attack from without had failed. But Balaam made an effort to earn his fee. He suggested a strategy which he felt might lead God to curse Israel against His will! Balaam reasoned that God could not bless a sinning people—and so he recommended that Balak attempt to corrupt Israel.

Protected from enemies within (Num. 25). Chapter 25 begins, "While Israel dwelt in Shittim the people began to play the harlot with the daughters of Moab. These invited the people to the sacrifices of their gods, and the people ate, and bowed down to their gods." As in most religions of Canaan, ritual prostitution was an intrinsic part of the religion of Moab.

This strategy which introduced sin into Israel is said in Numbers 31 to have been developed "by the counsel of Balaam" (vs. 16). Certainly a holy God would not bless a sinning people!

154

As in the past, God's anger was now focused on His people. But now the sin was dealt with in a way which showed a distinct change in the character of Israel. The leaders who had linked themselves with the Baal (a Semitic word meaning "lord" and designating false gods(were put to death by the people. However, because they were still impure, a plague struck Israel until a priest named Phinehas personally executed an Israelite and the Moabite prostitute he had brought into the very camp of Israel (25:7, 8).

It was by self-discipline—by the people of Israel choosing to purify themselves—that sin within was now being dealt with. The new generation was demonstrating its difference from the old. The choice to follow God was being made—and the cost of self-discipline being paid. Protected from enemies without and cleansed by self-discipline within, the people of Israel were demonstrating their readiness to receive the gift of rest.

EXPECTATION!

Numbers 26–36

The old generation is gone now, the last of them carried away in the plague of Baalpeor. Some 600,000 men are numbered:[7] the new generation matches in numbers their fathers, who by now have all fallen in the wilderness (26:64-66).

With the old generation gone, a new spirit takes

[7]This does not include the 23,000 Levites. See Num. 26:51, 62.

possession of Israel. In fellowship with God, sure of divine protection, the people look forward with optimism to victory.

This is shown strikingly in Numbers 27. Before a single battle for Palestine has been fought, five women appeared before Moses. Their father had died in the wilderness without sons. They felt that it would be unfair if their family had no possession in the land, even though no son lived to inherit. How striking this faith is! They never questioned the ultimate victory of Israel. They looked beyond the warfare to the time when the land would be divided among God's people. They expected so firmly to inherit the land that they treated it as though they were already in possession.

God's protected people have a right to this kind of optimism. We can look ahead with total assurance to promised victory.

And so we trace Israel's experience of victory in these last few chapters in Numbers. Poised on the edge of the Land of Promise, certain of victory, the new generation looks to the future with confidence in themselves and in their God.

HISTORY REVIEWED

Deuteronomy 1-4

The years of wandering are over now. Poised on the borders of Palestine, Israel's history is reviewed by Moses. Just as we did at the beginning of this chapter, Moses leads Israel to recall the history of their redemption. And now he speaks to a people who *do* trust God. "You who held fast to the Lord your God," he says, "are all alive this day" (4:4). A, purified people are ready to respond—and to know the great truth that sets them free. God's redeemed people are a protected people. "Know therefore this day," says Moses in words that echo in our own time, "and lay it to your heart, that the Lord is God in heaven above and on the earth beneath; there is no other" (4:39).

The Lord is our God.

As His people, we rejoice in Him.

GOING DEEPER

to personalize

1. Read the following chapters to get a feel for this section of Scripture: Numbers 21, 27, 31, 32.

2. Study the story of Baalam, and note especially the blessings pronounced on Israel by the unwilling prophet (Num. 22—24). Jot down any questions you have about these chapters for class discussion.

3. Skim Deuteronomy 1—4, reading *carefully* Deuteronomy 4. What truths in this chapter do you believe would have been particularly meaningful to Israel as they paused before entering the land?

4. How are the things you selected in 3 above (as being important for Israel) important for you?

to probe

1. Do a character study of Balaam, using materi-

al in these chapters and in the New Testament (see a concordance).

2. The tribes of Reuben and Gad chose to take their inheritance in trans-Jordan (Num. 32). How did their actions show that they viewed themselves as a protected people (cf. esp. 32:16, 17)? From what these two groups affirm, do a character study contrasting the old and the new generations.

11

OUR LIVING HERITAGE

YESTERDAY ONE OF THE neighborhood children went to court. The judge warned him: Once more, and you'll be locked up. That very afternoon, after a long session with my wife, the same 13-year-old stole money from our car to buy a birthday present. And that evening insisted, "Mom doesn't really love me."

Our young friend desperately needs love. But he's constantly testing the limits, constantly pushing to see how far he goes before he is rejected. Sure that he's not loved, he is also driven to prove over and over again that he is right about his unloveliness. When he is rejected or disciplined, he can confirm what he has accepted as his own tragic identity.

I have another friend who was brought up in a home without love. Married now, she is unable to express love to her husband in meaningful ways.

The cause has been traced and understood. But the void lovelessness has left in her personality has scarred her and, against her will, has hurt others as well.

The effects of a lack of love have been noted and traced by generations of psychologists—and myriads of sufferers. Some substitute food for affection, and grow fat. Others feel worthless, unable to value a personality their parents rejected. Still others are driven to prove themselves and try to earn love by accomplishments that stretch their nerves and energies to the breaking point. No wonder social psychologist Abraham Maslow places a need for "love and belongingness" as a basic need of the human personality, a need which must be met if a person is to grow toward becoming his potential self.

"Do I belong (acceptance)?" and "Am I loved?" are perhaps two of the most basic questions that can be asked in thinking about *any* relationship. It's not surprising, then, to realize that these basic questions are answered for Israel in an unmistakable way. Moses, speaking to a new generation of Hebrews about to cross the Jordan and take possession of the Promised Land, brings into clearest focus God's great assurance, "You are loved!" (Deut. 7:7, 8). The heritage of the Jews was not just a land. The heritage of the Jews was a living heritage— God Himself, walking in personal relationship with them.

Sometimes you too feel unloved and unaccepted. So do I. But something both of us need to do is to learn that we *are* loved: "When my father and my mother forsake me, then the Lord will take me up" (Ps. 27:10, KJV). As we look through these vital chapters of Deuteronomy, let's remember that these same affirmations of love are made to you and me. We too have a living heritage in our personal relationship with God through Jesus Christ. In Him we are accepted. And we are loved.

LOVED, AND LOVING

Deuteronomy 5, 6

In Deuteronomy 4 Moses explains God's deliverance of this generation's parents from Egypt this way: "because he loved your fathers [referring to Abraham, Isaac, and Jacob] and chose their descendants after them, and brought you out of Egypt with his own presence, by his great power" (4:37). The love God had for these men, who lived on in their descendants, led to a deep commitment on God's part that extended across the centuries.

But in chapter 5 we see a new and striking emphasis. Moses moves from history to Israel's *now*. He insists that God seeks relationship "not with our fathers" with whom the Law covenant was made "but with us, who are all of us here alive this day" (vs. 3). It is this relationship with "us, who are all of us here alive this day," that these next chapters of Scripture help us understand.

The nature of the relationship (Deut. 5). Several elements of relationship with God are defined here.

161

(1) *It is personal (5:1-3)*. The relationship is between "us, who are ... here alive," and Jehovah, who is also here and living. Often a person grows up in a home where the Lord is God of his parents. His relationship with God is through mom and dad; he goes to church because they do. This falls short of a love relationship. One who cares for us wants to reach out and touch us personally, not through others. God wants to know and love us personally, warmly, intimately—with nothing and no one between.

(2) *It is urgent (5:4-14)*. The urgency of the relationship is emphasized in the first four of the Ten Commandments, all of which are repeated here from Exodus 20. God wants our eyes fixed on Him. As any lover, He is unwilling to share our affection with competitors.

It's hard to imagine a husband who truly loves his wife unaffected by unfaithfulness or encouraging her to date around. Truly intimate love is to be exclusive. God wants and helps us to love other persons (even as a good husband/wife relationship enriches the context of the home for their children). But God will not share us with other gods—whether they be the idols of the ancient world or the financial success of the modern.

How comforting this is. God cares enough to be jealous. We really are important to Him.

(3) *It is demonstrated (5:15)*. Love that lets us feel our belongingness is demonstrated. How clearly God had demonstrated to this generation His personal and practical involvement with them: "God

brought you out thence with a mighty hand and an outstretched arm."

Christ is the ultimate demonstration of God's love for us. But each of us can find many other special ways in which God has acted in our lives to show His love.

(4) *It is expressive (5:16-20).* It is hard to feel loved when we don't really know what is going on inside a person who claims to love us. In this restatement of the last six of the Ten Commandments, we see God's willingness to communicate His expectations. This communication was first heard at Sinai with fear, but also with a certain responsiveness that pleased the Lord. "All that the Lord our God will speak to you," the people told Moses, "we will hear and do it" (vs. 27).

Love communicates and expresses; love desires a response. What is even more significant for us in our relationship with God is this: God wants to help us grow in our own capacity to love. As we saw earlier, these manward commandments are rooted in God's own concern for men. As we listen to Him, and respond to Him, we grow in our ability to love others.

This is an important thing to see. A person who loves another desires to see him grow. We can be utterly sure that God loves us because His every word to us is designed to help us grow to our full potential.

(5) *It is unselfish (5:29-33).* This last element of real love is affirmed in these verses. God enters into relationship with us, and speaks to us "that it might

go well with" us. As verse 33 summarizes, "You shall walk in all the way which the Lord your God has commanded you, that you may live, and that it may go well with you, and that you may live long in the land which you shall possess."

People who come into personal relationship with God are not pawns in some great game He is playing. God's love for us is unselfish. He honestly has our best interests at heart.

All of this helped Israel realize that it did have a personal relationship with the Lord, and that God truly did care. This people was loved. And so are we.

Perhaps your parents, or your spouse, have never let you know how deeply you are loved. Perhaps they haven't truly cared. But through Christ you can have a personal relationship with God Himself, in which you are loved and do belong. Personally, urgently, practically, expressively, unselfishly, God Himself says to you and me today: "I do care!"

The communication of relationship (Deut. 6). The people of Israel who stood on the plains across the Jordan and heard Moses' words knew they were true—from personal experience. Many of them had as children or youths seen God's acts of judgment on Egypt which freed Israel. All had eaten the manna, followed the fiery cloud, known victory over Moab, and seen many, many other evidences of God's personal presence and concern.

But when this generation crossed the river Jordan many things would change. The manna would cease, and they would eat the corn of the land. The cloud that guided them before would be gone. Victories would be won, but the supernatural evidences of God's presence would no longer be as visible. This generation knew—and Moses' words in Deuteronomy 5 must have brought the knowledge to full consciousness—that they were a special and deeply loved people.

How then would they communicate the reality of God and the love relationship they had with Him to the next generations? How do we help others know that God loves them personally? How do we help others enter into our heritage?

(1) *God's priority affirmed (6:1-9)*. The reality of God's love for us can only be communicated by those who give Him priority. Central to it all is, "You shall love the Lord your God with all your heart" (vs. 5). This love leads to a unique life-style; in the framework of our life-style the reality of God is communicated.

First, the lover of God responds to God. God's words are to be "upon [his] heart." This means that the Word of God becomes a part of the personality, that the divine values reshape the human values. Second, what has become of supreme importance is to be shared with others. "You shall teach them [God's words] diligently to your children" speaks not only of the parent's responsibility for nurture. It points up that the "you/your" relationship (a *personal* relationship) between human beings is vital if the *personalness* of the God/man relationship is to be shared. Here, in the daily activities of which life is constituted, God's words are to be shared with others. If we share His words with those who share our lives, the reality and the personalness of God will be known.

(2) *God's presence assumed (6:10-19).* Here we read of promises and injunctions which are to comfort and reassure Israel in the land. The whole tone is one of expectation: God will be with them, even though the signs have ceased. In this context verse 16 is especially significant: "You shall not put the Lord your God to the test, as you tested him at Massah." In this incident, recorded in Exodus, the people had rejected the signs of God's presence and challenged, "Is the Lord among us, or not?" The lesson is clear. Believers are to assume God's presence, knowing that He has promised never to leave or forsake us.

Sometimes we must take His love on faith. When others see us rejoicing in God's love in spite of circumstances, they too will perceive that He is real.

(3) *God's provision assured (6:20-25).* In such a relationship with the Lord, there will be only one answer when "in time to come" sons ask their fathers, "What is the meaning . . . ?" (vs. 20). Then the parents are to remind the children of God's action in delivering Israel from Egypt. Then too God is to be glorified as the One who provided the land of promise—and who provides for His people in that land.

In the context, then, of a personal relationship with God's children, who themselves have given God priority, trusted Him to be present, and experienced His provision, the reality of God's love can be communicated to others.

Ultimately this is the only way.

We can tell others about God.

We can even lead them to agree with God's Word.

But to bring them to know Him as a God who loves and who welcomes them, we need more. We need to identify ourselves with them and love them as God Himself loves us. How thrilling to know that we are loved by God. How thrilling to be freed by Him to love others.

OUR HERITAGE IS LOVE

Deuteronomy 7–11

Reading through these next chapters is an enriching and freeing experience. For God continually affirms His love for us. In fact, there is no better way to sense the affection God is pouring out than to let His Word speak for itself.

Deuteronomy 7. Once in the land, Israel is to destroy the pagans and their images, lest they draw God's people away from Him. Every alternative to a life of godliness is to be rejected. Why?

The Lord your God has chosen you to be a people for his own possession, out of all the peoples that are on the face of the earth. It was not because you were more in number than any other people that the Lord set his love upon you and chose you, for you were the fewest of all peoples; but it is because the Lord loves you, and is keeping the oath which he swore to your fathers . . . Know therefore that the Lord your God is God, the faithful God who keeps covenant and steadfast love with those who love him and keep his commandments, to a thousand generations (7:6-9).

Deuteronomy 8. Here God reviews His discipline of the unresponsive generation. What a purpose that discipline had—and how accompanied it was by love! Why did God discipline? "That he might make you know that man does not live by bread alone, but that man lives by everything that proceeds out of the mouth of the Lord. Your clothing did not wear out upon you, and your foot did not swell, these forty years. Know then in your heart that, as a man disciplines his son, the Lord your God disciplines you" (8:3-5). Every stroke of suffering was administered in love.

Deuteronomy 9, 10. Israel is again promised full possession of the land. But with the promise comes a warning. "Do not say in your heart, after the Lord your God has thrust them out before you, 'It is because of my righteousness that the Lord has brought me in to possess this land' " (9:4).

Israel is then reminded of its history of unresponsiveness and warned. Then, in touching words, God again shows how deeply He loves this people, though they have been rebellious. In an extended and touching section, the place of love in

God's action and the role love is to play in their new life-style is reaffirmed.

And now, Israel, what does the Lord your God require of you, but to fear the Lord your God, to walk in all his ways, to love him, to serve the Lord your God with all your heart and with all your soul, and to keep the commandments and statutes of the Lord, which I command you this day for your good. Behold, to the Lord your God belong the heaven and the heaven of heavens, the earth with all that is in it; yet the Lord set his heart in love upon your fathers and chose their descendants after them, you above all peoples, as at this day. Circumcise therefore the foreskin of your heart, and be no longer stubborn. For the Lord your God is God of gods and Lord of lords, the great, the mighty, and the terrible God, who is not partial and takes no bribe. He executes justice for the fatherless and the widow, and loves the sojourner, giving him food and clothing. Love the sojourner therefore; for you were sojourners in the land of Egypt. You shall fear the Lord your God; you shall serve him and cleave to him, and by his name you shall swear. He is your praise; he is your God, who has done for you these great and terrible things which your eyes have seen. Your fathers went down to Egypt seventy persons; and now the Lord your God has made you as the stars of heaven for multitude. *Deuteronomy 10:12-22*

Chapter 11 states the conclusion: "You shall therefore love the Lord your God" (11:1).

Love, because you are loved.

Respond, because God has acted for you.

Lay up God's words in your heart—because God has laid you on His heart. And you are loved. Loved and loving.

This too is part of redemption's message. Out of slavery, into freedom, growing through discipline to finally understand. God loves us. God accepts us. He has chosen us to be His own. You and I stand secure, surrounded by the love of God.

GOING DEEPER

to personalize

1. How have you felt loved (or the need to be loved) in your own life? How have either of these affected your personality? Jot down your insights about yourself and your background.

2. Imagine yourself to be one of the people of Israel to whom the words in Deuteronomy 5—11 were being spoken. Read Deuteronomy 7 as if you were there, hearing these words spoken to you. How would they lead you to feel about your relationship with God? About yourself as a worthwhile person?

3. Read Deuteronomy 10:12-22 (reproduced on p. 169 of the text). Underline (in the text or in your Bibles) statements which you believe God is saying to you now, as well as to Israel.

What do these affirmations and statements of His expectations mean to you?

to probe

1. Read the entire seven chapters (5—11), and mark in your own Bibles the following: (a) evidences of God's love for Israel; (b) indications of how Israel is to respond.

2. From your study of (1) above, write a two-page discussion on "the nature of love."

3. Compare this section of Deuteronomy with what Jesus says in John 15. Write a two- to four-page paper on the parallels.

4. Keep working to memorize the chart on pages 150, 151. You will need to be able to think through these books of the Old Testament for mastery of content and message.

DESTINY AHEAD

TWENTY YEARS AGO A traveler taking a train across Palestine remarked, "And the Bible calls this a land of 'milk and honey'!" A man overheard him, tapped him on the shoulder, and pointed him to these words in Deuteronomy 29:22-24:

And the generation to come, your children who rise up after you, and the foreigner who comes from a far land, would say, when they see the afflictions of that land and the sicknesses with which the Lord has made it sick—the whole land brimstone and salt, and a burnt-out waste, unsown, and growing nothing, where no grass can sprout, an overthrow like that of Sodom and Gomorrah, Admah and Zeboiim, which the Lord overthrew in his anger and wrath—yea, all the nations would say, "Why has the Lord done thus to this land?"

The Land of Promise, once rich and fertile, was destined to become a waste.

If . . .

COMMITMENT

Earlier, when Israel stood poised at Paran and sent spies to examine Canaan, the people had faced an existential choice. God spoke a single word: Go. And they refused.

On this decision the destiny of an entire generation hinged. Because of their lack of trust in God, their decision was to disobey. We have seen how that single act of disobedience—representative of a basic attitude and life-style—forced them out away from the Promised Land to die in the wilderness.

But now we are reading of a new generation, a generation which did "hold fast" to the Lord. This generation is ready and eager to respond to the command to cross the Jordan and enter the battle for their heritage, Palestine. This new generation has a different heart attitude toward God, and is marked by a different life-style. They are a people who trust God, and who are willing to obey. But they too now face a decisive decision. This decision must express itself not in a single act of obedience or disobedience, but in a continuing pattern of life.

The decision Israel now faced had to do with commitment.

New Testament parallel. We can find a similar point of decision reflected in the Gospels. Jesus had spent a long time with His disciples, and a similar length of time in ministry to the crowds. Then He asked the twelve, "Who do the crowds say I am?"

He received many answers. John the Baptist. Elijah. Others of the old-time prophets.

And then the Lord asked, "Who do you say I am?"

And He received the right answer. "The Christ of God." The disciples knew who He was, and trusted themselves to Him. They had made that critical initial decision to respond to God's Word about His Son, even as the believing Israel had made a critical initial decision to respond to God's Word and go up into Canaan.

But that initial decision, important as it is, must be followed up. Jesus said to His disciples:

> If anyone would come after me, he must deny himself and take up his cross daily and follow me. For whoever wants to save his life will lose it, but whoever loses his life for me will save it. What good is it for a man to gain the whole world, and yet lose or forfeit his very self?
> *Luke 9:23, 24*

In these words Jesus sets before believers the second choice: the choice of commitment. Jesus is spelling out the ultimate impact of that choice on the human personality. If we choose to follow Jesus in daily commitment, we will "save" our lives. We will become the self we potentially are through the presence of God's life within (see pp. 56 and 57). Or we can make the wrong choice. We can live for ourselves rather than in commitment to Christ. An inevitable result of that choice will be that we lose ourselves. The person we might have been because of a relationship with God—our "very self"—will be forfeited.

Commitment determines the destiny ahead in this world for each of us.

For Israel too. It is a commitment decision that faces Israel now as well. Just as Christ spoke to His disciples—and through those words speaks to us today—so Moses spoke to the new generation ready for conquest, and through those words spoke to succeeding generations of Jews. In these critical chapters of Deuteronomy, God carefully defines the commitment He expects, and He thoroughly explains the impact of whatever choice His people might ultimately make.

As we trace the culminating events in Deuteronomy, we see over and over again how the commitment decision determines the experience of Israel. Ultimately the Messiah-King will come, and all of God's promises to Abraham will be fulfilled. But until then, each generation's choice will determine its own destiny.

DEUTERONOMY 12—26

The opening chapters of Deuteronomy affirmed God's love for Israel. Never could they look at His commands or discipline as cold and unfeeling. Israel could rest secure in the confidence that God truly cared.

The middle chapters of the book are a restatement of the Law. This is, of course, the source of the book's title: Deutero- (second) -nomy (Law). We need to remember when we read it, should it seem repetitious, that this restatement is to a new generation. And it is actually more than just a restatement. Deuteronomy is the document of the covenant that this new generation was to enter into with God once they had taken possession of the land (Deut. 11:29; 27:1-8; Josh. 8:30-35).

Not all the Law is restated. But many elements are.

The warnings against idolatry.

The law of the tithe.

The Year of Jubilee, and the year of release for the poor.

The appointments for the feasts.

The administration of justice.

Laws concerning chastity and other case-law types of injunction.

The offerings of the firstfruits.

All the elements of Israel's way of life—from worship to social and civil guidelines—are reviewed for a generation called on to make that decisive choice concerning a way of life.

BLESSING AND CURSE

Deuteronomy 27–30

Covenant entered. It seems strange to read words like these in this section of Deuteronomy: "This day

you have become the people of the Lord your God"
(27:9). That is, it would seem strange if we failed to
remember that the Mosaic covenant is an existential
covenant. The Hebrews, as a people and as individuals, chose to enter into that relationship with
God defined by the Law (review chs. 5 and 6 of
this book). The promise made to Abraham held
firm no matter what a given generation might do.
But each generation's own experience of God's
blessing, and their own relationship with the Lord,
was defined by the Law and entered into by their
choice. Thus the Deuteronomy passage we are
studying picks this critical point in time to explain
for Israel for all time the meaning of such a commitment decision. "You stand this day all of you
before the Lord your God," Moses proclaimed,
"that you may enter into a sworn covenant of the
Lord your God, which the Lord your God makes
with you this day; that he may establish you this day
as his people . . ." (29:10, 12).

To mark off this day as special, an appropriate
ceremony was determined. Israel was told to act out
her commitment in an unmistakable way. When
she was over Jordan, the commandments were to
be written plainly on large, whitewashed stones.
Half the tribes were to stand on Mount Ebal, and
shout out "Amen" to the curses pronounced by the
Levites upon disobedience (cf. 27:15-26). The
other half of the tribes were to stand on Mount
Gerazim to bless. And an altar was to be built—on
the mount of cursing.

Thus commitment was to be marked formally in

the experience and the memory of the Israelites.

Commitment defined. The definition of commitment given here is extremely simple.

Daily obedience.

We see it over and over, "If you obey the voice of the Lord your God, being careful to do all his commandments which I command you this day . . ." (28:1).

It is just as simple to define lack of commitment, or uncommitment.

Daily disobedience.

"If you are not careful to do all the words of this law which are written in this book, that you may fear this glorious and awful name . . ." (28:58).

The decision the believer makes is to live out his commitment to God as daily obedience—or not to.

Fulfillment. This is the outcome of the commitment, for the nation and for the individual. We see it clearly in these chapters.

Obedience brought blessing. There would be an increase of crops and cattle in the land. Israel's undertakings would prosper. They would be victorious in warfare. God promised, "The Lord will establish you as a people holy to himself, as he has sworn to you, if you keep the commandments of the Lord your God, and walk in his ways. And all the peoples of the earth shall see that you are called by the name of the Lord" (28:9, 10).

In serving the Lord "with joyfulness and gladness of heart" (28:47) Israel would find fulfillment.

Destiny. The men and women Moses spoke to that day across the Jordan did move out to live a life of

179

commitment. Their lifetime was marked by just the blessings God promised. Theirs was an experience of fulfillment.

But their descendants, of whom Moses also was speaking through the written word, did not respond. They turned from serving God, and the very experiences so graphically described in these passages became in fact the history of which we read in the remainder of the Old Testament. The destiny ahead for Israel was described, and the pivot on which future history would turn defined. At every point in Israel's history—and in our own personal destiny—the issue is one and the same: commitment.

What was the future against which Israel was futilely warned?

The Lord will bring on you and your offspring extraordinary afflictions, afflictions severe and lasting, and sicknesses grievous and lasting. And he will bring upon you again all the diseases of Egypt, which you were afraid of; and they shall cleave to you. Every sickness also, and every affliction which is not recorded in the book of this law, the Lord will bring upon you, until you are destroyed. Whereas you were as the stars of heaven for multitude, you shall be left few in number; because you did not obey the voice of the Lord your God. And as the Lord took delight in doing you good and multiplying you, so the Lord will take delight in bringing ruin upon you and destroying you;

180

and you shall be plucked off the land which you are entering to take possession of it. And the Lord will scatter you among all peoples, from one end of the earth to the other; and there you shall serve other gods, of wood and stone, which neither you nor your fathers have known. And among these nations you shall find no ease, and there shall be no rest for the sole of your foot; but the Lord will give you there a trembling heart, and failing eyes, and a languishing soul; your life shall hang in doubt before you; night and day you shall be in dread, and have no assurance of your life."

Deuteronomy 28:59-66.

The land of milk and honey, of fulfillment and promise, would also bear the judgment, to become a "burnt-out waste."

And this is just what has happened.

The destiny written as warning so long ago has become history. The word was true. The danger inherent in the rejection of commitment is real.

RETURN

Deuteronomy 30

Along with the warning God gave a promise. Even in the middle of judgment, if the blessings and the cursings would be called to mind, and God's people "return to the Lord your God . . . and obey his voice in all that I command you this day,

181

with all your heart and with all your soul; then the Lord your God will restore your fortunes, and have compassion upon you, and he will gather you again from all the peoples where the Lord your God has scattered you" (30:2-3).

The invitation to commitment is an open invitation. It is never too late for the believer to return to God. The door remains open to the people of God. All God asks is that we respond to Him. "I have set before you this day life and good, death and evil," comes His living Word. "If you obey the commandments of the Lord your God which I command you this day, by loving the Lord your God, by walking in his ways . . . then you shall live and multiply. . . . But if your heart turns away, and you will not hear . . ." (Deut. 30:15-17).

Then destiny will most surely become history.

So Jesus' words echo an age-old story. The person who will not follow his Lord may gain a world, but he forfeits himself. What he could have become he will not, even as Israel's choices would lead her to forfeit the blessings of the Promised Land.

GOING DEEPER

to personalize

1. Read through Deuteronomy 27—30, underlining verses or sections which seem particularly significant to you.

2. The author suggests that there is a parallel between the choice of commitment which God

through Moses gives Israel, and which Christ specifies for His disciples.

Make your own chart, showing as many parallels as you can between the two calls to commitment.

3. In Deuteronomy 28 and 29 God carefully specifies for Israel just what lack of commitment would bring. Write your own description of the life an individual believer today might expect if he chooses to live an uncommitted life. (Remember that the blessings and the cursings will not be the same for individuals today as for the nation Israel. Your clue: What are the blessings in the New Testament God promises to work in individuals who trust Christ and grow in Him?)

4. Some might see "legalism" in the stress on obedience here and in other Old Testament passages. How, from Deuteronomy 30, would you specifically refute this notion? Try to write out a two-page answer.

to probe

1. From your previous knowledge of the Old Testament, make a chart of Israel's history from Sinai to Christ. Be as detailed as possible in your outline.

Then study these chapters very carefully. Can you match what you read here with Israel's actual history?

Spend enough time on this study to do a thorough and careful job of correlation.

183

COMMISSIONED

THE BOOK OF DEUTERONOMY closes on an intensely personal note. The Lord says to Moses, "Behold, the days approach when you must die; call Joshua, and present yourselves in the tent of meeting, that I may commission him" (31:14).

Here, looking back on the jolting series of events that ripped Israel from slavery, thrust her into a wilderness where she could learn to become the special people of God, and now brought her welded together into a unified nation, we realize perhaps for the first time how dominant one man has been in this history. God has done the work. But clearly He chose to do His work through a man, Moses.

As the days of the Exodus draw to a close, the divine benediction pronounced on Moses in the two closing verses of Deuteronomy are clearly appropriate. "And there has not arisen a prophet since in Israel like Moses, whom the Lord knew face to face, none like him for all the signs and the wonders which the Lord sent him to do in the land of Egypt, to Pharaoh and to all his servants and to all his land, and for all the mighty power and all the great and terrible deeds which Moses wrought in the sight of all Israel" (Deut. 34:10-12).

The very uniqueness of Moses makes it hard for us to study his life. How can we identify with him?

Today you and I as Christians are believer-priests. It's true that we have been given spiritual gifts, and commissioned to serve God and others. But we can hardly identify the Body of Christ, the Church, with the nation which came out of Egypt. So we hesitate before we proclaim Moses as the model of leadership on which to pattern pastoral leadership (or leadership of a committee or small group Bible study or a Sunday school department). "There has not arisen a prophet since in Israel like Moses" is a warning that we need to take seriously.

And yet God is speaking to us through Moses. The uniqueness of the task which God set for Moses warns us not to take him as a pattern for all leadership. But the fact that Moses was a man, like you and me, means that we can learn from him. Looking at Moses the man we can see a model for relationship with God that will help us fulfill our own call, whatever that call may be. While Moses' mission was unique, his humanity was something we all have in common with him. It is in identifying with Moses the man and learning from him how a commissioned man related to the God who called him that we find our greatest personal encouragement and aid. The lessons that Moses learned so well are just the lessons you and I need to learn, whatever our own mission may be.

MAKING OF THE MAN

Exodus 2–5

Scripture gives us an unmatched picture of the formative decades of Moses' life. With the possible exception of David, no other Old Testament individual is so clearly portrayed. With Moses, as with David, we're struck first of all that God took years to prepare the man for his ministry. For Moses, God spent 80 years shaping and molding in order that 40 years could be dedicated to service.

Sometimes we're in too great a rush to get into God's work. First God molds men. Then He uses them.

It's clear that a number of processes were being worked out in Moses during these long and formative decades.

Opportunities to use (Ex. 2): the palace. God placed Moses in a unique position. One of a slave people, he was adopted and taken into the palace of Pharaoh. He took advantage of this opportunity. Acts 7 tells us, "Moses was educated in all the wisdom of the Egyptians and was powerful in speech and action" (Acts 7:22).

This is an important object lesson for us. We need to use every opportunity God gives us to grow as persons, and to develop within our own culture. Personal enrichment is not merely for our own sakes—it is a course we undertake for the ultimate glory of God.

Dreams to dream (Ex. 2): the dead Egyptian. Exodus 2:11 tells us that when Moses was about 40 he "went out to his people and looked on their burdens." For all his accomplishments in the Egyptian culture, Moses still looked upon the slaves as "his" people! There, seeing a slave mistreated by a taskmaster, Moses killed the Egyptian. Stephen, speaking in Acts under the inspiration of the Holy Spirit, reports, "Moses thought that his own people would realize that God was using him to rescue them" (Acts 7:25).

Moses was dreaming a dream. He envisioned himself as one God would use to deliver Israel.

Not all of us are called to fulfill our early dreams. But to desire great things for God, and to dare great things to help those about whom God cares, are valid for us as well.

Discipline to accept (Ex. 2): the flight. The Jews did not share Moses' vision of himself as hero. Word was passed to Pharaoh of his intervention for the slaves, and "Moses fled from Pharaoh." For 40 years he then lived as a shepherd in a backward land. His dreams of Moses-as-hero faded under the constant and repetitious toil as a shepherd. As a prince Moses had dreamed great dreams; as a poor working man, Moses accepted himself as a "nobody."

We all need this kind of discipline. Not that our

spirit or our faith might be broken, but that our dreams might be tempered by awareness of our essential "nobodyness." We are all important because of what we can do. But it is when we accept ourselves as loved and valued, yet at the same time unimportant, that we can be used. At some time each person God uses must become a nobody. Only then can God act to make him a somebody.

Limitations to face (Ex. 3, 4): the burning bush. Moses evidently carried his nobodyness too far. When, at 80, God spoke to him out of the burning bush and announced that his youthful dream would be fulfilled, Moses hesitated. Now he saw many reasons why he could not do what he had once planned to do.

"They will not believe me."

"Lord, I am not eloquent."

"Lord, send, I pray, some other person."

All these objections indicate clearly that Moses now was all too aware of his inadequacy. From "I can" he had swung to "I can't."

It's important that we face our limitations and reject all trust in our natural abilities or skills. But we can be too overwhelmed by our weaknesses. Now God had to shift Moses' gaze from himself to his Lord.

Commissioning to accept (Ex. 3, 4): the call. In the call to Moses God had announced His purposes. "I will send you . . . that you may bring forth my people, . . . Israel, out of Egypt" (3:10). For each objection God had a promise:

"They will hearken to your voice."

189

"Go, and I will be with your mouth and teach you what you shall speak."

God is well able to do in us what He intends. With the commission comes the promise of God's presence and His power.

Disappointments to face (Ex. 5): fresh burdens. Moses went. As God had said, the Hebrews did believe Moses and welcomed him. But, as God had also warned, Pharaoh would not listen. The burdens of the slave race were increased. The people of Israel turned on Moses, and Moses turned to the Lord. "Why hast thou done evil to this people? Why didst thou ever send me?"

This is part of our preparation too. In every ministry there are disappointments to face. All doesn't go as we wished (and God even warns us to expect initial setbacks).

Learning to accept disappointments and to always turn to God is an important phase of preparation for any ministry.

These early chapters, then, focus our attention on lessons the believer needs to learn as preparation for whatever ministry God may call him to. They are as applicable for the Christian parent or businessman as for the world-renowned evangelist. Each of us is called to use our opportunities to grow as persons, to catch a vision of the greatness our relationship with God implies, to accept that disciplining which teaches nobodyness and helps us face our limitations. Each of us too is called to realize that when God calls and commissions us, the promise of His presence means that our limitations will

190

be overcome. In His strength we can step out, face initial disappointments, and grow into that stature needed to fulfill our personal call.

THE BURDEN OF MINISTRY

Exodus 15–40

The events immediately following the exhilarating confrontation with Pharaoh take us far beyond Moses' preparation and thrust us deeply into discovering the burdens of spiritual leadership. The early days of head-to-head conflict with Pharaoh, of miraculous judgments taking place at Moses' word, must have been exciting. But the months of excitement soon passed. The glamour faded. The thrill of victory disappeared under day-to-day routine and repeated problems.

Moses' basic problem was with the people he had been called to lead. Very quickly their character was revealed. When Pharaoh followed them to the sea they turned on Moses and in fear begged to be allowed to return to slavery (14:11, 12). Even after the great victory there, within three days we see Israel "murmuring against Moses" because of a lack of water (15:22-24). As the journey progressed, the attitude of the people continued to sour. The "whole congregation" murmured (16:2), and finally expressed their rebelliousness in an anger so great they were ready to stone Moses himself (17:4).

As we look at Moses the man we need to see him

191

as one who is constantly under such pressure. Being a leader means carrying a very real and very heavy burden. Any kind of ministry means bearing the burden of others. In the context of Moses' experience, we can find insights into how we are to face and overcome the burdens that come with our own ministry call.

Not alone (Ex. 17, 18): the recognition of others. Under the pressures we've just seen above, Moses quickly came to the end of himself. Exodus 17:4 portrays him crying out, "What shall I do with this people?"

What a fascinating cry. "What shall *I* do?" Moses was about to learn a vital lesson. He had looked at himself as one who had to provide all solutions. Moses saw himself not only as isolated, but as indispensable.

"What shall *I* do?" is often the cry of the ordained minister in our churches today. Somehow pastor and people feel that ministry is one man's responsibility, and one man's alone. No wonder it sometimes seems impossible.

It is!

Ministry was never meant to be a one-man operation. Even the ministry of Moses, a unique leader who is clearly the central figure in God's work at this time in history, was not to be a one-man show. How much less is leadership in the Body of Christ, a people who are all gifted by the Holy Spirit, to be autocratic, or to exalt one man.

God responded, "Pass on before the people, taking with you some of the elders of Israel" (17:5).

God then told Moses to strike a rock. "Behold, I will stand before you . . . ," God said, "and water shall come out of it."

Here are two ways in which Moses was not alone. God was there before him. And some of the elders of Israel were there with him.

This lesson of the role of others was reinforced in the events which immediately followed. As Israel traveled on, they met an enemy, the Amalekites. Joshua led Israel to battle, and whenever Moses held up his arms, outstretched over the battlefield, Israel won. But Moses' arms became tired. He could not hold them up alone. And when he lowered his arms, Israel lost. There was only one solution. Moses sat on a rock, and Aaron and Hur stood beside him and held up Moses' arms.

What a clear message for Moses. Moses was unable to provide for God's people alone. He had to have others beside him.

In chapter 18 we see the culmination of this lesson. Moses, the lonely leader, is still trying to do it all himself. So all day long he must sit and settle disputes that arise among the people. His father-in-law, Jethro, visited him and saw what was happening. Jethro then broke in, "Why do you sit alone, and all the people stand about you from morning till evening?" (18:14). Moses explained: "They come to me to inquire of God." Jethro's comment was as potent for us today as it was for Moses. "What you are doing is not good. You and the people with you will wear yourselves out . . . you are not able to perform it alone."

Now Moses heard. Moses chose capable men, and delegated authority to them (18:24-27). Hard cases were still brought to Moses. But these men now judged the common cases themselves.

Ministry is to be shared among God's people. Even when those people are not yet grown to maturity, the leader is not to bear the burden alone. Whatever your call is, you are not alone.

And you are never to make the mistake of thinking that you are the only one God can use. The lesson Moses was taught is meaningful for us today as well.

Interceding (Ex. 32): the golden calf. It's fascinating to read Exodus 32. Moses was on Mount Sinai receiving instruction from God. Down in the valley, Israel had reverted to type. Under pressure from the people, Aaron had weakly given in and made a golden calf for them to worship. God now tells Moses what has happened, and invites intercession with these words: "Now therefore let me alone, that my wrath may burn hot against them . . . but of you I will make a great nation" (32:10). God expressed His own commitment to judge sin, and offered Moses an even greater place in history than he now filled. Moses' response?

He prayed.

In the striking prayer recorded in Exodus 32:11-14 Moses called on God to glorify Himself by remembering His covenant promises to Abraham. Moses was looking to God and seeking His glory. He wanted to see God glorified in His people, and to this end he prayed for them.

God responded to Moses' intercession. The guilty individuals would die . . . but the nation would live.

And when Moses returned to camp? The Bible says "[when he] saw the calf and the dancing, Moses' anger burned hot, and he threw the tables out of his hands, and broke them . . ." (vs. 19). When Moses saw what the people were doing, he reacted as God had—with anger! An angry Moses could never have prayed with that same concern as had the Moses on the mount.

This too teaches us.

In our ministry we will see much which might appropriately anger or disgust us. Yet Moses when his eyes were fixed on the Lord was invited to intercede, and did intercede with a view to the ultimate glory of God. We too are to intercede with our eyes on God, and with a concern that all which angers Him might be dealt with by transformation, not destruction. The New Testament says it. "The wrath of man does not work the righteousness of God." Keeping close to the Lord Himself, we will be protected, as Moses was, from an anger which might keep us from helping others. By keeping close to the Lord, we will also rely on Him and express our concern for others in prayer.

A LONG LIFE

Numbers, Deuteronomy

For 40 years Moses led Israel. And 38 of those

years were spent in leading a doomed generation through the wilderness . . . waiting. Two incidents selected from Exodus (from many possible ones) have helped us see something of the lesson Moses learned of ministry's burdens. The Book of Numbers helps us realize that leaders bear a limited responsibility.

In many ways Moses seems to have been a failure. He failed to bring Israel into the land. He saw the generation he brought out of Egypt wander aimlessly in the desert, doomed to die. He saw little change in their responsiveness to God or to himself.

Was Moses to blame? In Numbers 13 and 14 we read of Moses and the people hearing the report of the spies about the strength of Canaan. In terror Israel refused to move into the land. The Bible tells us that "Moses and Aaron fell on their faces before all the assembly of the congregation." In horror, with Joshua and Caleb, they begged the people to respond to God.

But the people would not.

In Deuteronomy we read of Moses bringing a new generation to a similar point of decision. The last two verses particularly are words that point up the necessity of choice.

Strikingly, all the Book of Deuteronomy, a great and long discourse by Moses, is designed to bring the people of Israel to this point of decision. Moses reminds the new generation of victories won (chs. 1—4). He stresses the love God has for them as His people (chs. 5—11). He outlines again key points in the Law that will bring them blessing and justice (chs. 12—26). Finally he faces them with the need to choose (chs. 27—30). But Moses did not choose for them. He could not. The people had to choose for themselves.

There are limits to the responsibility of leaders. These are imposed by the very freedom God Himself gives all men to turn to Him—or else to turn away.

Moses' ministry was designed to bring men to the point of decision. He performed that ministry well.

One generation turned away from God.

One generation turned to God.

To both these generations Moses' ministry had been the same. It was not Moses' fault or Moses' failure when the men he was commissioned to lead refused to respond.

And it was not because of Moses' skill that he had success with a second generation.

The point is simple. Moses was called to be faithful to God in fulfilling his commission. He was not called to "succeed" or to "fail"! And so come the words of commendation found in the New Testament: "Moses . . . faithfully discharged his duty in the household of God" (Heb. 3:2, Phillips). It was Moses' faithfulness to his task which counted with God all along.

And it is the same for us today. Where there is faithfulness, failure does not bring blame. And success does not bring glory. Our responsibility is limited. We are called merely to bring others to the place where they can choose.

MORE

Yes, much more. A whole book, rather than just a chapter, might well be devoted to Moses the man. We could trace his humanity, and see the little weaknesses which show up in each one of us. We could study his prayers, and see in them both his deep need for God and the frustrations he felt because of his inadequacy. We could examine his sin—a sin that kept him from entering with Israel the land that had been his lifelong goal.

· But perhaps even more significant is the fact that in each of our personal journeys down freedom road we share the life both of the nation—and of the man who led it. Redemption's road leads us, as we take the step of commitment, on to ministry. As we grow in our own understanding and experience of redemption, we find that, like Moses, we, too, are commissioned. Commissioned to grow and develop our own potential as persons. Commissioned then to bear the burden of others, suffering with them and for them. Commissioned to be faithful in bringing them ultimately to the place where they too will be able to choose.

Able to choose to travel with us, down freedom road.

GOING DEEPER

Before going on to the next book in this Bible Alive series, take time to review these four books of the Old Testament and see what additional lessons God wants to teach you through Moses the man.

You might want to start with a striking lesson about prayer. It's found in Numbers 11. When the people of Israel complained about Moses, Moses' response was to complain to God! See if you can discern why the people's refusal to blame God is viewed as a rejection of Him—and why Moses' immediate response of finding fault with the Lord (vss. 10-15) was not rejection. What does this mean for you? Study the passage, and see.

FIGURE XI

I. PRIMEVAL PERIOD	CREATION Creation to Abraham	*Genesis 1–11* *Job*
II. PATRIARCHAL PERIOD (2166-1446)*	COVENANT Abraham to Moses	*Genesis 12–50*
III. EXODUS PERIOD (1446-1406)	**LAW** **Moses' Leadership**	***Exodus*** ***Numbers*** ***Leviticus*** ***Deuteronomy***
IV. CONQUEST OF CANAAN (1406-1390)	CONQUEST Joshua's Leadership	*Joshua*
V. TIME OF JUDGES (1367-1050)	JUDGES No Leadership	*Judges* *Ruth* *I Samuel 1–7*
VI. UNITED KINGDOM (1050-931)	KINGDOM Monarchy Established Establishment (David) Decline (Solomon)	*I Samuel 8–11* *II Samuel 1–24* *I Kings 1–11* *I Chronicles* *II Chronicles* *Psalms* *Ecclesiastes* *Proverbs* *Song of Solomon*

*The dates are taken from *A Survey of Israel's History* by Leon Wood (Grand Rapids: Zondervan, 1975).

VII. DIVIDED KINGDOM (931-722) Israel Elijah Elisha Judah	PROPHETIC MOVEMENT Two Kingdoms	*I Kings 12–22* *II Kings 1–17* *II Chronicles 10–29* *Jonah* *Obadiah* *Amos* *Hosea* *Micah* *Joel* *Isaiah*
VIII. SURVIVING KINGDOM (722-586)	Judah Remains	*II Kings 18–25* *II Chronicles 30–36* *Jeremiah* *Nahum* *Zephaniah* *Habakkuk*
IX. BABYLONIAN CAPTIVITY (586-538)	JUDGMENT Torn from Palestine	*Ezekiel* *Daniel* *Esther*
X. RESTORATION (538-400)	The Jews Return 400 Years Between the Testaments	*Ezra* *Nehemiah* *Haggai* *Zechariah* *Malachi*

FREEDOM ROAD

THE NATURE OF BIBLE SURVEY

BIBLE SURVEY IS NOT Old Testament introduction. Introduction courses tend to focus on details about the Bible. They explore authorship, examine arguments for canonicity of books, struggle with dating, and argue for or against such things as the J, E, D, P documentary hypothesis or a Deutero-Isaiah. Certainly issues an introductory course deals with are important, but survey is not primarily concerned with them.

Bible survey is not apologetics either. It is not primarily concerned with the defense of some view of Scripture, or with resolving some historical or philosophical problem. Courses in apologetics also tend to talk about the Bible: to spend time comparing Bible documents with similar content from comparative cultures, etc. Apologetics has a place, but not in survey.

Nor is Bible survey a series of sermons. There does need to be some element of application in any study of the Bible, for the Word of God does speak to us as individuals. But survey goes beyond the development of application. Survey focuses on mastery of the Scripture and of its significant messages.

In the most significant sense, Bible survey brings us to a study of the content of the Bible. We are not primarily concerned with what men say about the Bible: we are concerned about what the Bible says. It is the text itself, what God is saying to us, that we are eager to master. What God says and His message to us are always the orienting thrust in Bible survey. It may, for instance, be interesting to debate the early or late date of the Exodus, and rethink the arguments that lead us to pick Hatshepsut as the princess who rescued the baby Moses. But such argument is something we set aside in Bible survey. We do not go into detail in order that we may concentrate on the main teachings and the message of each Bible portion. Our goal in survey is that our students might know what God is saying in each major section of the Bible, and that they might hear what He is saying to them today.

What then is the value of a survey approach?

■ *We give students a foundation for a lifetime of Bible study.* Survey provides initial acquaintance with the whole Bible, an acquaintance that opens up the Bible for in-depth study to follow.

■ *We give an orientation to Scripture's sweep and theme.* Too many believers today are Biblically ignorant. They do not know how the Bible fits together; they do not know its major themes and emphases; they are particularly confused by what they read in the

Old Testament. Survey helps "put the Bible together."

■ *We place vital tools in believers' hands.* Someone who knows how the Bible fits together is able to interpret it more accurately than one who grabs at a verse and applies it without knowing the historical setting or the purpose of God when that word was first spoken. When we understand what God's Word meant to the men and women of the day in which it was spoken, we can apply it to ourselves with greater confidence.

Each of these benefits can be ours when we come to the Word of God to master its content and listen to its message. And each of these benefits will be ours as we work through the Old Testament portion of our Bible survey. In these studies you'll give your students insight into the sweep and the significance of Old Testament history. You'll give your students a mastery of the Bible that enables them to relate people and events and revealed truths to periods of God's progressive revelation. You'll give your students a grasp of the purpose and the place of each book in the time when it was written. And you'll help them hear God's message: you'll give students an appreciation for the major themes, the relevance, and the use for today of each Old Testament book. Finally, you will see God use His Word. Scripture's word does speak to us today. In our Bible survey studies we will hear God's voice—and be drawn into a closer relationship with Him.

APPROACHES TO SURVEY

THERE ARE SEVERAL WAYS to approach Bible survey studies. One way is thematic: taking a topic like "salvation" and tracing it through the entire Old Testament, then moving to another topic like "sin" and doing the same thing. A second approach to survey is to focus on groupings of books: the Pentateuch, the Poetical books, the Minor Prophets, etc. Another approach is dispensational: to look at periods when God seems to be dealing with men in certain ways that differ from His ways of dealing at other times. (For instance, Adam was not under the Law. He really had no Ten Commandments to live by.)

The approach we'll take in the **Bible Alive Series** is different from each of these. Our approach is based on the flow of Bible history. This is important for several reasons. First, God's revelation did take place gradually, over many centuries of time. What God revealed was progressively unfolded. Jeremiah, for instance, learned more of God's Covenant purpose than David had known; David learned more than had been shown to Abraham. We want to trace the unfolding of God's plan and purposes as the unfolding happened; we want to understand teachings and truths and events in their developmental sequence.

Second, God's revelation was focused on contemporary needs. God spoke to living generations of believers, communicating the word they needed then. When we understand the crises which stimulated the communication of particular truths, and the historical situation into which the revelation came, we have important insights into the meaning of the written Word for us in our day.

Third, the books of the Old and New Testaments do not appear in our Bibles in the sequence in which they were written. We need to place them in order, and see clearly the process of history if we are to understand clearly God's Word.

For these major reasons, and others, our approach in these survey studies will be to explore God's Book in a sequence determined by Bible history. We will examine each of the ten periods of Old Testament history, and the Old Testament writings associated with them. To help your students master the Old Testament, you'll want to suggest they memorize the ten periods, and the data that appear on the chart (pp. 200, 201). The particular period or periods covered in this book of the **Bible Alive Series** are in bold-face type.

Dating. Just one word about the dating given on the chart in this series. There is, of course, disagreement among scholars about some of the dates for specific Bible events. I have accepted the dating system in Leon Wood's excellent book, *A Survey of Israel's History* (Zondervan, 1970), as representative of the best of conservative scholarship. If you wish to explore the reasons behind dates given, you can refer to his careful documentation and reasoning.

TEACHING BIBLE SURVEY

YOUR GOAL IN TEACHING Bible survey is to help your students master both the content of Scripture and its message. You want them to interact with the Bible, not just to read the textbook or listen to your lecture.

Teaching survey means motivating and guiding a class to dig into the Word of God, and then to explore together what it says and what it means. How do the resources provided in the **Bible Alive Series** help you?

The Bible. Most of your students' reading will be done in the Bible itself. Help them select a good modern version, one that won't confuse or cloud the meaning by using archaic English. You may want one of the modern paraphrases (such as *The Living Bible*), or you may want to stick with a good translation, such as the new *New American Standard Bible* or the *Revised Standard Version*. Encourage all your class members to use the same version, but invite them to check others when questions of interpretation arise. Most of your discussion in class should focus on the Biblical text itself, and on discoveries your students have made in reading God's Word.

The textbooks. This book, and each book in the **Bible Alive Series**, is designed to lead your students into the Bible. Each chapter in the text organizes a distinct segment of Scripture (sometimes a chapter, sometimes many chapters) in a way that will help your students fit that section together and also will sensitize them to the central message of that part of the Word.

The **Bible Alive** texts are not commentaries designed to cover the whole Bible. Instead each is written to orient the learner to the Bible section being studied, and to encourage him to move into the Word to make his own discoveries within the framework provided.

Often, when large sections of the Bible are being discussed in a chapter, students will be asked to read only parts of that section of their Bibles. The passages the class is directed to read are either *representative passages* (which enable them to sample a larger segment) or *significant passages* (in which critical teaching or revelation is given). By using the textbooks to orient the reader to the scope and general meaning of a section of Scripture, and then focusing his attention for more intensive study of a representative or significant part of that section, maximum value for study time is assured. (Thus, for instance, we will not ask students to read the whole Book of Leviticus. Instead, several chapters that bring into focus specific emphases of that book will be assigned.)

The textbook, then, provides a framework for fruitful Bible study, and goes on to guide that study.

Assignments. Each chapter in the text suggests two kinds of assignment. The first type involves reading and thinking which personalize the message of Scripture. These assignments are designed to help the learner meet God as He speaks to him through His Word today. Whether your students are members of a weekly Sunday school class or are in a course given for credit in college or seminary, you'll want to take time to work through the personalized studies.

Additional assignment suggestions are given with each chapter which help the student taking a credit course to probe beyond what might be expected of the less academic Bible student. As the teacher you may, of course, give any or all of these activities as assignments, or may develop comparable assignments of your own. It is important, however, in the credit course as well as the Sunday school or home Bible class, to make sure that your students study the Scriptures for growth and for enrichment, not just to gain information or pass examinations.

The class itself. Your time together in the class is important, particularly because, through discussions and various other teaching approaches, you can help your students think deeply about what they have studied in Scripture and its meaning for them today.

There is also a place, of course, for lecture, and for input of your own ideas and research. The lesson plans provided suggest appropriate topics and resources for short lectures; you'll have material of your own you feel is important as well. But in my own teaching of Bible survey on a graduate level, I found that helping the truths of the Word come alive to my students was the most vital part of the course. So the lesson plans emphasize some of the

FIGURE I

USE OF RESOURCES

The Bible: • the primary textbook; most time is to be spent in direct Bible study

The text: • gives a framework for direct Bible study

• guides the student to explore representative or significant passages

• suggests assignments for personal Bible study

The class: • helps students share discoveries

• allows learning activities to stimulate understanding and application of Bible portions read

• lets teacher add significant input, clarify, guide

Teacher supplement: • suggests teaching goals for each session

• suggests teaching methods for each class session

• gives sample quizzes and exams

methods I used then, as well as the lectures (which now are, in large part, found in the chapters of the text).

Quizzes and exams. Quizzes and examinations are an important part of this course, not as a basis for grades, but as an element of the learning process. Good quizzes and examinations are designed to help the student see just how much he has learned, and to motivate him for further study. Poor quizzes and exams are often designed to find out what the student has not learned—and to penalize him for his lack.

In a very real way, the only test of success in Bible teaching is related to the learner's response to God's Word long after he has left the class. Bible survey is designed to motivate further Bible study. If in later years our students become true explorers of the riches of God's Word, we have succeeded. If, as we are studying together, our students are responding to God as He speaks to them, then, too, we will have evidence of success. The ability to pass an examination is evidence neither of your success as a teacher nor of the student's success as a student of God's Word. For this reason, our quizzes and tests are designed to give positive evidence of significant learning, to motivate and to encourage the student, and to focus for him what is important to master.

These "success" (not "easy") quizzes and tests are also included for your use if desired.

THEN . . . AND NOW

WHETHER YOU ARE CONTINUING with a regular class in Old Testament survey, and moving on from *Let Day Begin* (the **Bible Alive** study in Genesis), or just beginning this study of Old Testament redemption with a new group, it's important to take time to help your learners identify with the Biblical generation they'll be studying. If our contemporaries are to hear the Old Testament as God's message to us today, they need to see their likeness to men and women of old. So take time this first class session to set the interpersonal stage. It's vital to your survey of these key Old Testament books.

It may be that your students will already have had the chance to read the text and study Exodus 1—4 before this class. Or perhaps you'll be giving out the textbooks after this first session. Select and adapt the teaching suggestions to your own situation.

LAUNCHING

Select one of more of the following:

1. Introduce students to each other by having each give his first name and tell one trait he admires in some Bible character. Have each tell why he finds this particular trait important to him.
2. Continuing classes might be divided into smaller study groups. Half of them should study Exodus 1 and 2 to develop a character sketch of the enslaved Israelites. The other half should study Exodus 3 and 4 to develop a character sketch of Moses. After 15 or 20 minutes, pull the groups together to compare.
3. Or you might introduce these studies by a survey of how Israel came to be in Egypt. Use material from the text (chap. 1). Other good sources for content are: *Moses and the Gods of Egypt,* Bolton Davidheiser, Baker, and *His Way Out,* Bernard Ramm, Regal. Each is a paperback.
4. Sketch the plight of the Israelites under the Pharaohs, and ask your students to jot down two "feeling" words which describe how the Hebrews might have felt in their bondage. Then ask your students to meet in groups of four and describe a time when they felt as the Israelites must have.

INPUT

Select one or more of the following:

1. If you chose *Launching* (1) or (2) above, give a

ten-minute lecture capsulizing the historical situation, and telling why God led His people into this experience. Do not mention the fourth reason, "the experience of suffering," yet.

2. If you chose *Launching* (3), follow up now with either the expression of "feeling" words (4, above) or with the character studies (2, above).
3. Another option, if your students have studied the text and the Bible passage before class period, is to put on the chalkboard a large chart to represent Moses' life (see *personalize* 2, p. 22 of the text). The chart might look something like this.

FIGURE II

MOSES' LIFELINE

Following discussion of the value of these ups and downs in shaping Moses' character, have your students break into groups of five to draw—and share—personal lifeline charts (see *personalize* 3, p. 22 of text). You'll want to launch this study by sharing a chart of your own lifeline, and letting the class question you if they wish. This setting of the example is vital to effective Bible teaching (Lk. 6:40), and will help others on to more meaningful sharing.

IMPACT

This final activity is the one in which you want to complete your students' sense of identity with God's Old Testament people, and motivate them for the studies in these Old Testament books. Probably this is the best way: real aloud the "experience of suffering" section of the text (pp. 17-19). Ask your students to record on a sheet of paper an area of their lives in which they sense bondage. Promise that no one will read what they record.

When this is completed, point out that our studies in these four Old Testament books (Exodus, Leviticus, Numbers, and Deuteronomy) not only tell of the initial redemption of God's Old Testament people from bondage, but go on to trace how that redemption was applied until it resulted in victory.

Sometimes we tend to think that salvation is the end of life's pilgrimage: that after we come to God, all will be easy. Actually the Bible indicates that salvation is the beginning of our pilgrimage. The challenge facing all of us is to learn how to apply the salvation God offers us creatively as we live out our lives.

Freedom Road shows us how to do just that:

how to apply salvation and experience its benefits as we come to better understand the meaning of our redemption.

To understand redemption is to find freedom. What your students have written is the very best of reasons to look forward to your studies together as an exciting—and important—adventure.

ASSIGNMENT: Text, chapter 2; selected *Going Deeper* items.

NOTE: Before going on in this course, you will want to read the discussion of testing and grading on pages 276-286.

CONFRONTATION!

THIS PASSAGE OF SCRIPTURE will generate many questions. What of God's act in "hardening" Pharaoh? What were the plagues of Egypt really like?

The first question is hard to resolve, having been the focus of long theological debate. Let your students probe it. Any who are really concerned might do a paper on the subject for extra credit.

Leon Wood's book, *A Survey of Israel's History*, goes in detail into the times and dates of the period. Dr. Wood develops some fascinating and relevant material. You may wish to select some for inclusion in your lectures.

You'll want to keep explanations of each of these questions subordinate to the emphasis of the Scriptures themselves. This emphasis is on a fresh and new revelation of God as "One who is always here," active in the present experience of His people.

LAUNCHING

Select one or more of the following:

1. Divide your class into interest groups around the two speculative questions suggested above. Let one group share opinions on "What was God's hardening of Pharaoh?" and the other group on "What were the plagues on Egypt?" After 15 minutes or so, call the class together, and let them raise questions with you for another ten minutes. You'll want to prepare for this carefully.
2. Hold an "open question" forum, in which you invite your students to raise any questions they wish about the text. If you do select this option, warn your class ahead of time.

By handling questions at the beginning of class, you'll be able to spend the rest of your time concentrating on the more critical issue.

INPUT

There are many different topics you might like to research for a mini-lecture: the length of time Israel was in Egypt; the Egyptian religious system; background on the plagues; etc. If you do choose to give a mini-lecture today, hold it to ten minutes.

IMPACT

Today focus on the message of this passage, using more of the following approaches:

1. Put a three-section chart on the chalkboard: one section labeled past, the others present and future. Ask your class to fill in together what they know about God that fits in each category. See how much of their understanding is past and future, how little in the present work of Christ in our lives. Then discuss the meaning of "Jehovah."
2. Ask your students to share the results of their study of the *personalize* 1 assignment on page 39 of the text. Then move on to *personalize* 2.

ASSIGNMENT: Read text, chapter 3, do selected *Going Deeper* items.

LIFE FROM DEATH

SOMETHING INTERESTING HAPPENS IN Bible teaching when we concentrate our attention on the *meaning* of the passages of Scripture studied. What happens? Students learn facts. My own name for it is "hidden learning."

We shouldn't be surprised. Data and details are best retained when set in a framework of meaning. It's harder to learn long lists of numbers or words by rote than it is to master similar lists when items are linked by a common element or meaning.

Too often Bible teaching focuses on mastery of detail apart from meaning. It's then that the Bible seems to some to be a dry and dull book. But when we seek to master the developing thought of Scripture, and to see the divine purpose and planning which link all its recorded events, the Bible comes alive. In focusing on meaning, we learn an amazing number of facts.

Bring this hidden learning home to your students. It's good for them to see how much they are learning without "studying" or memorizing lists. When I was teaching I often used quizzes—totally unannounced and unexpected—to help my classes realize how much they were learning. Maybe you'll want to try this technique too. I've included a typical quiz, to which you can add items if you wish, as this session's Launching activity.

LAUNCHING

a surprise quiz to reveal "hidden learning"

The questions on this quiz cover the first 15 chapters of Exodus. They are the most difficult of all questions, demanding recall without such hints as are always present in multiple choice and true/false questions. Yet your students will be able to do surprisingly well—even though they have made no effort to memorize class notes or the text.

1. Outline the major periods in Moses' life.
2. Give two of the four reasons the text suggests that Egypt was in God's plan for Israel.
3. What key word or thought indicates the central message of each of the following passages:
    Exodus 1—4
    Exodus 5—11
    Exodus12—15
4. List five of the ten plagues God brought on Egypt.
5. Give two reasons why experiencing God's power to deliver was important for Israel at this point in its history.

226

6. What confrontations does Exodus 5—11 direct our attention to, and which is most important?
7. Explain the significance of the name Jehovah, and its emphasis in Exodus 6.
8. List four evidences that the Passover is a very significant historical event.
9. In one sentence, describe the relationship between the Passover and Jesus Christ.
10. Briefly describe the sequence of events reported in Exodus 14.

After giving this test (allow about 20 minutes), take time to work through the answers with your students, letting each correct his own paper.

INPUT

Select one or more of the following:

This lesson is one which focuses on very significant content. So take time to give at least one lecture survey from the following:

1. Trace the Bible's teaching about sacrifice through the Old Testament. Be sure to begin in Genesis 3 with God's sacrifice of animals to obtain skins to cover the sinning pair. It is important that your students see sacrifice as a consistent Biblical theme—not a ritual "picked up" by the Hebrews from pagan cultures.
2. You might want to outline Israel's festival system.
3. Or you might trace in class what the rest of the

FIGURE III

FESTIVAL SYSTEM

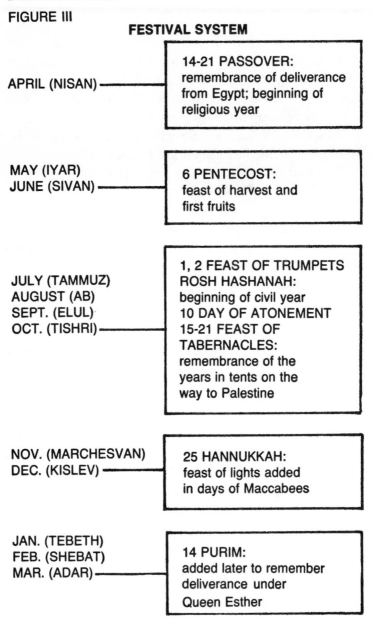

APRIL (NISAN) —
14-21 PASSOVER: remembrance of deliverance from Egypt; beginning of religious year

MAY (IYAR)
JUNE (SIVAN) —
6 PENTECOST: feast of harvest and first fruits

JULY (TAMMUZ)
AUGUST (AB)
SEPT. (ELUL)
OCT. (TISHRI) —
1, 2 FEAST OF TRUMPETS ROSH HASHANAH: beginning of civil year 10 DAY OF ATONEMENT 15-21 FEAST OF TABERNACLES: remembrance of the years in tents on the way to Palestine

NOV. (MARCHESVAN)
DEC. (KISLEV) —
25 HANNUKKAH: feast of lights added in days of Maccabees

JAN. (TEBETH)
FEB. (SHEBAT)
MAR. (ADAR) —
14 PURIM: added later to remember deliverance under Queen Esther

Old and New Testaments tell of the history of the Passover.

IMPACT

Select one or more of the following:

After the lecture on sacrifice, it is appropriate to conclude by discussing with your students their responses to the *Going Deeper personalize* studies 1 and 2. Or you might want to do an inductive study of Hebrews 10 together.

ASSIGNMENT: Text, chapter 4, and *Going Deeper* items.

Text, Chapter **4**

Exodus 15–20

DELIVERANCE AND DISCIPLINE

THE SUBJECT OF THE LAW is a vital one, basic to our understanding of the Old Testament. The Law guided and patterned Israel's way of life. The Law set Israel apart from the nations round about them. Israel was proud to be a people of the Law, even in their days of backsliding and sin.

But the people of the Law often misunderstood the nature and purpose of the Law. Even today, with the New Testament's expanded revelation of God's purposes, the place of the Law is often misunderstood. This lesson and the ones following it are extremely important. They develop, step by step, an insight into the Law which is in harmony with God's total revelation through both Testaments, and which is basic to our students' grasp of Scripture.

LAUNCHING

Select one or more of the following:

Whichever approach you choose, you'll want to look ahead to make sure that you don't move too quickly in this session. Working toward understanding of the Law should proceed slowly, a step at a time.

1. Explore your students' feelings about the Law. Ask the class to jot down words that express their feelings when told: "you've got to," or "you ought to."

   List the feelings on the chalkboard. You'll find a variety of both positive and negative words included. Talk about why the different kinds of feelings appear.

2. With the class make a chart diagraming God's acts and Israel's reactions on the journey to Sinai (Ex. 15—18). Then ask your class to share their own portraits of Israel's "personality" as they came to Sinai (*personalize* 3, p. 67).

INPUT

1. If you plan to use approach 1 in *Impact*, give a mini-lecture on the Law's function in helping the believer know God as a Person. You may want to use passages like Psalm 19 or 119.

2. You may want to go into some detail here about the nature of the Law Covenant as compared with similar covenants from the ancient world. Stress both the similarities and the dramatic differences which commentators delineate.

232

FIGURE IV

ISRAEL	GOD
Praise (15:1-21).	Sea opens for Israel, destroys Egyptians (14:30).
3 days later: "Murmur against Moses." No water (15:22-4).	God gives fresh water (15:25).
45 days: "Whole congregation murmurs against Moses" (16:1-3). etc.	God gives bread and meat (16:13-15)

3. Discuss if you wish the analogy of Israel at this time in history to the early days of a child's life. You may want to suggest parallels beside those drawn in the text.

IMPACT

Select one or more of the following:

1. Now approach the topic of the Law as a revelation of God's character. Ask your class members to take turns completing the following statement: The commandment_____ (fill in one of the Ten) tells me that God (values,

233

cares about, is concerned about, etc.)
_____. Go around the circle as many
times as you can, recording the suggestions of
each class member.
2. Examine Hebrews 12:5-13 together, noting the
commitment of God to discipline those whom
He loves. After talking about this text in its rela-
tion to Exodus, encourage your students to talk
about times they have experienced God's discipline. Encourage them to draw parallels between their experiences and those of Israel.

ASSIGNMENT: Text, chapter 5, and selected
Going Deeper items.

THE BEGINNING OF WISDOM

THIS SECOND OF THREE CHAPTERS on the Old Testament Mosaic Law has two major emphases. First, it seeks to help your students understand the Law as being in full harmony with love. It is not a case of "be loving" *or* "keep the commandments." The Old Testament message is "Love God and others *by* keeping God's laws."

The second emphasis prepares for the next chapter by pointing up several distinctives about the Law Covenant as contrasted to the other Biblical covenants. These differences need to be highlighted. They lay a basis for understanding that the Law system was intended to be a temporary system, to be superseded when Christ came.

You may wish to combine lessons 5 and 6 in a single class session. Decide now.

LAUNCHING

Begin this week with a quiz. Select four or five

samples of case law from Exodus 20—24 or Leviticus 19. Put the verses on the chalkboard, and ask your students to quickly write down (a) how this item expresses love and (b) how it provided God's people with freedom.

For instance, you might select Leviticus 19:9, 10: "When you reap the harvest of your land, you shall not reap your field to its very border, neither shall you gather the gleanings after your harvest. And you shall not strip your vineyard bare, neither shall you gather the fallen grapes of your vineyard; you shall leave them for the poor and for the sojourner."

Clearly this statute teaches consideration for others. What's more, it protects the pride of the poor, who were given rights—not charity. It also provides for the integrity of the poor in that they were to go and glean, they themselves thus meeting their own needs by their own effort. In many ways freedom is protected: the wealthy are freed from greed, the poor from humiliation. Each man can hold his head high. None can look down on another.

You will, of course, also want to include at least one of the more difficult injunctions in the five.

After your class has taken a few minutes to work on their task, spend at least 20 minutes talking over these situations, helping them suggest and see some of the many implications involved.

(By the way, Deuteronomy 8:11 helps us see some of the reason behind the specifically religious case laws. These were part of a pattern of life in which the Hebrew could not "forget the Lord!")

INPUT

Select one or more of the following:

1. Discuss the chart on page 79 of the text. You may want to have your class look at Joshua 24:14-28. This illustrates the awareness of the leader Joshua of a need to bring the new generation to acceptance for themselves of the Law's covenant obligations. Later in history, and today, the Bar Mitzvah ceremony introduces children into the Covenant as a member with adult responsibilities, continuing to demonstrate the conditional and two-party nature of the Mosaic Covenant.
2. Review the four points made on pages 75-78 of the text. You may want to introduce the chart found in chapter 6 of the text, showing the relationships between the Biblical covenants at this point. A preview of this aspect of the next chapter might be valuable here.

IMPACT

Select one or more of the following:

1. Have your class brainstorm for a list of at least 50 statements about the Mosaic Law. They can use what has been studied, what they have heard others say, etc. Statements can be either True, or False, or Uncertain. After the list is completed, work through it evaluating the accuracy

of the statements on the basis of what you've discovered in the study of Exodus 19—24 to date.
2. Or discuss *probe* 1, from pages 80, 81.

ASSIGNMENT: Text, chapter 6; do selected *Going Deeper* items.

BEYOND THE LAW

THIS SESSION STEPS BEYOND the Old Testament framework of our studies to summarize key teachings of the New Testament. Law/Grace is one of those topics which invites far more exhaustive treatment than we can give it here. (It will be developed more completely when our survey studies bring us to Romans and Galatians in the New Testament series.) Probably the best way to handle this section is to give a series of mini-lectures on key points. Then open the class for discussion.

For this session, then, I have suggested several different lecture elements from which you can select—or which you can use in total.

INPUT

Select one or more of the following:

Each of the following is supplementary to, and

239

does not duplicate, content given in the students' text. You may wish to discuss the content there, as well.

1. *Law's temporary reign*

Figure TS 6 shows a timeline of Old and New Testament in outline, showing that the principle of promise (cf. Gal. 3:15-18) runs through the Old and New Testament, antedating the Law and never set aside by it.

FIGURE V

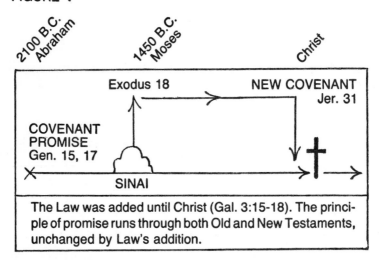

The Law was added until Christ (Gal. 3:15-18). The principle of promise runs through both Old and New Testaments, unchanged by Law's addition.

2. *Law to be replaced*

Jeremiah 31:31-35 promises that the Mosaic (Law) Covenant will be set aside when God makes a New Covenant with Israel. Note particularly the specific aspects stressed:

   a. The New Covenant is to be unlike the Mosaic.

b. The New Covenant, like the Abrahamic, is to be unconditional—not conditional.
c. The New Covenant focuses on the inner man rather than on behavior. Under the new system the principles of righteousness expressed outwardly in the Law will be written "upon their hearts" as character.
d. Complete forgiveness is an essential aspect of this New Covenant approach. Point out that Scripture makes it very clear that God always remains concerned with righteousness. When we move beyond the Law we find that same concern, but expressed in a different—more effective—way (Cf. Gal. 5:13-26). The New Covenant, of course, was made at Calvary; the blood of that Covenant was Christ's (Heb. 9:15-20).

3. *Events at Sinai*
The sequence of the events at Sinai themselves demonstrate the fact that the Law was never intended as a way of salvation, or of providing righteousness.

Camped at Sinai	Exodus 19—Numbers 10
Law Given	Ex. 19—24
Tabernacle Established	Ex. 24—40
Instructions for Holy Living	Lev. 1—27
Camp Organized	Num. 1—10

The Law was given first, bringing Israel to an

awareness of sin. Immediately afterward a system of priests and sacrifices, focused in the Tabernacle, was established. This system defined how a sinner could approach a holy God (through sacrifice) and provided access. Note, for instance, that the person entering the Tabernacle court passed through a single access gate, at which was the brazen altar of sacrifice. Only through the shedding of blood (cf. pp. 46-48, text) could one whom the Law condemned approach the Holy One of Israel.

God then went on to speak to a cleansed people and define the life-style appropriate to continual relationship with Him. The forgiven people are to grow in their relationship with the Lord. Finally the camp is organized: the people of God needed to be organized and disciplined if they were going to be able to live effectively in the world.

There are, of course, parallels here between Israel and the believer. After we recognize sin and come to Christ for forgiveness, we too need to grow in relationship with the Lord, and be equipped for our life in the world.

No one aware of this sequence and its implications could mistake the Law as a way of salvation.

4. *Focus on character*

It might be helpful for your students to compare and to contrast Exodus 21—24 with such passages as Ephesians 5:1-20 or Colossians 3:1-25. In these later passages righteousness is clearly of central concern. Yet the focus of exhortation is on inner attitudes and values.

In an earlier class we demonstrated how the Law itself revealed the values, through defining specific behaviors. Now the emphasis is directly on the inner values from which behavior springs.

The point of course is clear. Now God the Holy Spirit personally and directly guides our behavior each moment—in harmony with the values which God has planted both in our hearts and in His Word.

5. *A test case*
One final approach may be helpful. The Law stressed right behavior. When the New Testament moves beyond the Law, the change in approach is demonstrated in the way believers approach differences and problems. This is shown clearly in the way Paul handles the dispute recorded in I Corinthians 8. In this passage Paul resists discussing the problem on the basis of "right" or "wrong." He suggests instead that, while knowledge is always limited, love opens up persons to God and to each other. In this disputed case, each party needs to be careful in the exercise of its freedom to consider the conscience and welfare of brothers. Resistance to "giving the right answer," or to laying down rules, is characteristic of the way things are handled under Grace.

For a parallel passage, see Romans 14.

243

Summary. In this class your purpose has been to stretch your students to see that, while the Law is no longer to rule the believer's life as it did in Old Testament times, God is still concerned with righteousness. Discussion of some (or all) of the items sketched above will help your students see glimmerings of God's grand plan for us: a plan that goes beyond the Law.

ASSIGNMENT: Text, chapter 7. Selected *Going Deeper* items.

AN OPEN DOOR

THIS SESSION IS ANOTHER in which application should receive primary emphasis. Each believer has discovered that salvation has not brought adequacy. Christ put it this way: "Apart from me, ye can do nothing." The Tabernacle, coming historically as it did immediately after the Law had revealed sin, was a promise that God makes provision to meet the continuing need of His people.

The Tabernacle itself was placed in the middle of Israel's camp. The "tent of meeting" was a visible reminder of God's presence. And each article of furnishing held its own distinctive promise of provision.

So as you teach this session, help your students realize that in Christ we have the promise of the Tabernacle fulfilled. Christ Himself has taken up residence in the believer, and in His presence we have available now all the resources we need to live a holy life.

LAUNCHING

Select one or more of the following:

1. Give a quick review quiz, listing the following passages: Exodus 1—4; 5—11; 12—15; 15—20; 20—24. Ask your students to write beside each its message (see text, pp. 150, 151).
2. Ask your students to share, in groups of four or five, their "after salvation" ups and downs, which they were to chart for the *personalize* 1 assignment (p. 110).
3. Brainstorm with your whole class for "disappointments" which new Christians often experience. List your students' suggestions on the chalkboard. Focus in by discussing which seems most common, or most serious. Suggest that the Tabernacle study helps us see how God intends to meet these very needs of ours.
4. Start with a brief lecture. Stress how the events of Exodus 32—34 demonstrated the need of the redeemed people for release from sin's power. Stress parallels with Christians today and our need after salvation for continued deliverance. (Be sure your students understand the nature of *types*. See the discussion in ch. 12 of *Let Day Begin*, the first book of the **Bible Alive Series**.)

INPUT

Select one or more of the following:

1. Place the following chart on the chalkboard, leaving the last column blank. (It will be filled in

246

by your class as an Impact activity.) You may
wish to be ready with New Testament references which express the realities given in picture
form in the Tabernacle.

FIGURE VI

THE TABERNACLE

FURNISHING	SYMBOLISM	N. T. REALITY
Brazen Altar	Entrance de-mands sacrifice	Christ died to win us access
Brazen Laver	Those within need cleansing	etc.
Shewbread	All needed to strengthen and supply pro-vided daily	
Golden Candlestick	Light by which to see provided	
Golden Altar of Incense	Praise and prayer	
Ark of the Covenant	Presence of God	
Veil	Way into God's presence not open	

2. Select one article of furnishing in the Tabernacle and trace its New Testament fulfillment. For
instance, the candlestick speaks of the Holy

Spirit enlightening and guiding the believer. It also speaks of walking in the light (I John); the believer's privilege of understanding and doing God's will. A concordance study of "light" is very helpful here.

IMPACT

Select one or more of the following:

1. Let your students share what each feels God is saying to him through the Tabernacle *personalize* 3, p. 110).
2. Discuss insights and questions of your students generated by reading Exodus 35—40 (*personalize* 4).
3. Fill in the fourth column on the Tabernacle Chart (Fig. TS 7). Have your students match the resource pictured by each item of furniture with the "problems" brainstormed for Launching 3. For instance, a sense of weakness in facing temptation forces us to look to Christ as strengthener and sustainer, pictured in the table of shewbread. Encourage your students to share how they have experienced each ministry of Christ in their own lives. Be sure you share as well.
4. Read and explain Hebrews 9.

ASSIGNMENT: Text, chapter 8. *Going Deeper* items.

IN FELLOWSHIP

OUR SURVEY TOUCHES VERY lightly on the Book of Leviticus. Much of the material in this book relates so specifically to Israel that it is enough to know the message of the book, and how it fits into the history of redemption. What is important for us is that message: a redeemed people who have access to God through sacrifice are to live a distinctive, set-apart life. They are to be holy, with a holiness that is evident in their life style.

The priesthood, introduced in Exodus and constantly in focus in Leviticus, is another thing. Here we have a basic Old Testament institution that has continued importance for us. In understanding the priesthood, we come to a fresh appreciation of Christ's present ministry on our behalf. And we gain fresh insights into our own ministry as believers who have all been lifted to a role once reserved for only a few.

LAUNCHING

Select one or more of the following:

1. From Church history, give a ten-minute lecture on the role the doctrine of "the priesthood of all believers" had in the Protestant Reformation (particularly the Lutheran). Lead then into a discussion of whether Christians today understand and exercise their priesthood.
2. Set up a simple three-column chart on the chalkboard. In the first column record your students' suggestions of "past ministries of Christ" (in redeeming, in revealing God to us, in performing miracles, in creating, etc.). In the third column have your students suggest "future ministries of Christ" (that is, what will He do in His return?). In the center column ask them to suggest items to list reflecting Christ's *present* ministry. Chances are the first and third columns will contain many more items— pointing up our failure to grasp the practical meaning of Jesus' present high priestly ministry for us.
3. Give a "pop quiz" and have your students write briefly describing the content or message of one of the Leviticus chapters (see *personalize* 1, p. 125).
4. Begin the session by asking each student in turn to complete, aloud, the sentence: "Because Jesus is my High Priest, I _____" Record what each says on the chalkboard. Give your own contribution last.

INPUT

Select one or more of the following:

1. If you do not wish to focus on the priesthood in your class, you may want to go into more detail on the offerings (Lev. 1—7), the festivals (Lev. 23), and the Year of Jubilee (Lev. 25) which marked Israel's life as distinct. However, it is probably more important to focus on priesthood.

2. Develop your own lecture on the present work of Christ, or cover the entire high priestly work (including His sacrifice of Himself). Use books on Christology as your source; you'll need several to find sufficient material. You will want to emphasize Christ praying for us (cf., for instance, I Jn. 2:1, 2), His preparing a place for us (Jn. 14), His ministry of mediating forgiveness and cleansing (cf. Heb. 4:16), His ministry of sustaining and strengthening (with Heb. 4:16, recall His nature as "bread"), His guiding ministry as Head of each individual and the Church (Eph. 1:22; 4:15), etc.

Note the relationship here to the typical significance of the items of furniture in the Tabernacle. Every need is met by the present ministry of Jesus for us.

IMPACT

Select one or more of the following:

With the lecture emphasis on the priesthood of

251

Christ, it's appropriate for this interaction time to seek out the meaning of priesthood for believers today. Here are several possible approaches:

1. List the priestly ministries of Christ on the chalkboard, and ask your students to suggest parallel ministries (or corrolaries) for believers.
2. Do an inductive study as a group of II Corinthians 3:1-18. In this passage Paul speaks of believers as "ministers of a new covenant." The apostle thus is contrasting the priest who ministered under the Old (Mosaic) Covenant with the believer-priest who ministers under the New (Christic) Covenant.

Give your students ten minutes to look individually for correspondences and contrasts—and for indications of how our priesthood is fulfilled today.

Some of the contrasts they will notice:
Now God writes on hearts, not stone. The living person is "read" by all: we communicate Christ by who we are. We too "judge," but only as God Himself through the Spirit leads. (Note that the Old Testament priest made judgments on the basis of externals. Now we need to distinguish on other criteria entirely: I Cor. 2:14, 15.) The priests' clothing (covering) was their "beauty and glory"; believers remove veils for, while still vulnerable and human, we "are being transformed into his likeness with ever-increasing glory."
Some of the indications as to how we minister:

252

We communicate God's message by our lives. We accept identification with frail, imperfect humanity, yet God's work in our lives demonstrates His transforming presence. As a result others come to know Christ, and are themselves transformed (see also II Cor. 5:11-15).

3. Close today by going around the circle and having each person complete this sentence: "Because I am a believer-priest, I _____ "

ASSIGNMENT: Text, chapter 9, selected *Going Deeper* items.

THE CHOICE

THIS SESSION AGAIN PROVIDES a vital personal focus, emphasizing the need of your students to be responsive to God. So focus most of your class time on learning activities which will help your students apply the truths illustrated in this chapter.

Note that an "application" approach to teaching this passage is the one taken in Scripture itself. In both New Testament sections which comment on it, the focus is clearly on application.

LAUNCHING

Select one or more of the following:

These launching suggestions are designed to make sure that your students have grasped the message of this Old Testament segment. Once you are confident they have, you can move quickly on to exploring the message's meaning.

1. *Quiz.* Give your students eight minutes to scan

and then write a quick evaluation of Numbers 16. They should show how this incident fits the pattern of irresponsibility which Israel has established, and also how God sought to teach them to be responsible.

2. Have your students work in pairs to summarize "the most important thing I've learned from Numbers 1-20." They should take no more than four minutes, and write down as clear a statement as they can. Then have the pairs share their statements, record them on the chalkboard, and when all are in view, lead a ten-minute discussion on what in the passage illustrates or justifies these conclusions.

INPUT

It is probably best to turn here to the divine commentary found in Hebrews 3:7—4:11. Work through the passage by sections, tracing the argument which shows the lost generation's failure to enter God's rest because of a disobedience that was rooted in unbelief. Show too how the writer points out that we are faced with the same choice, with similar impact on our lives.*

IMPACT

Select one or more of the following:

There are a variety of ways to help your class

*For an extended discussion of this passage, see Larry Richards' book, *The Complete Christian,* a commentary on Hebrews, published by Scripture Press. Paper, $1.95.

explore the meaning of this truth for their own lives. Choose the approach or approaches which you feel will be most helpful in leading your class to share personal experiences as well as to talk about the concepts involved.

1. Discuss the story of Laura (text, pp. 129, 130). How does the lesson taught Israel in Numbers 1—20 apply to her situation? What are some of the parallels in the situation?
2. Ask your students to identify with Laura, and jot down a brief description of a time when each felt something like she must feel. When these descriptions are completed, break into groups of four or five to share them with others, and to report also what happened. How did the outcomes of the situations parallel—or differ from—outcomes in Israel?
3. Ask your students to turn to page 140 and to complete the right-hand side of the chart by writing in a description which characterizes the *pattern* of their lives. (We all fail to respond to God at times. But Israel made unresponsiveness and distrust a way of life. It is the life-style which is important here.)

    After this is done, fill in on the chalkboard two possible patterns, one of which could be reflected in any student's book. One pattern would duplicate Israel's. The other would be the reverse, and involve trust, obedience, rest. . . .

    Discuss each of these patterns, and how the results might show up in persons' lives. Be particularly ready to illustrate the practical meaning of rest (see *The Complete Christian*).

ASSIGNMENT: Text, chapter 10, selected *Going Deeper* items.

Note Especially: It is always important to have a *framework of mastery* when we approach Scripture. Our personal study is enriched if we are able to *think through* large sections of the Bible, knowing its progression and development and message as these are related to the whole. So be sure to have your students memorize the chart found on pages 150, 151 in the next chapter.

NO ENCHANTMENT AGAINST ISRAEL

AS YOU APPROACH THE end of this course, you'll want to make sure your students have mastered the framework of these Old Testament books and the message of each section. So take time this class period to work with your students on content mastery, using the chart on pages 150, 151 of the text. Take up to half the class period in memory activities.

For the rest of the period you may wish to focus on the story of Balaam and the incident at Peor (Num. 22—25) for principles of protection.

LAUNCHING

Select one or more of the following:

1. Have the chart of this period (pp. 150, 151) on the chalkboard as your students arrive ... but with *any ten of the spaces* blank. Have the students

work in pairs to fill in the chart without refer-
ring to the text. Then recognize the pair with
the most completions and the most accurate
answers.

2. When the students arrive, have them refer to
the chart on pages 150, 151. Note that the *Key
Verse* column is not completed. Ask your students, in pairs, to select a key verse for each
section. Assign each pair at least three sections.
After about ten minutes, call for reports. Have
each pair discuss and justify its selections.

INPUT

Because of the length of time the *Launching* activity
(s) should take this week, do not plan any lecture
inputs.

IMPACT

Select one or more of the following:

1. Discuss the blessings pronounced by Balaam on
Israel *(personalize* 2, p. 157). Let your students
raise any questions they may have about this incident.

2. Read Deuteronomy 4 in class, aloud. Ask your
class to stop you any time you read something
which they feel is especially significant for Israel
or for themselves. Discuss each insight as it is
shared.

3. Give a brief commentary on the principle of *expectation.* When the believer finally realizes his

protected position, he is uniquely freed to expect God's best in his life. We too can expect God to work in us.

ASSIGNMENT: Text, chapter 11, selected *Going Deeper* items. Also memorize half of the chart, pages 150, 151 (Ex. 1—40). Quiz next period.

OUR LIVING HERITAGE

THESE CHAPTERS OF DEUTERONOMY are especially vital for us today. They help us realize that the living God seeks a personal love relationship with men. They help us explore the nature of His love for us, and analyze our response.

Often, as the chapter introduction suggests, children grow up into youth and adulthood without knowing true love. The result is nearly always insecurity and uncertainty, an inability to trust others or themselves, and an inability to reach out and care.

Today we want to explore both what the Bible says about God's love for Israel, and what the certainty that God loves him can mean for each of your students. This then can be a critical session, one in which far more than content is communicated. It can be a time for individuals in your class to find their deepest needs beginning to be met—in a personal experience of the love of God.

LAUNCHING

Select one or more of the following:

1. Talk about the incidents reported in the introduction to the text's discussion (pp. 159-161). What other results of a failure to feel loved and accepted can your students think of? (Note: this may move into personal sharing. If so, encourage it, and share yourself.)

2. Divide the class into groups of four to share the insights gained by each individual into himself or herself (see *personalize* 1, p. 170).

3. Play a previously taped recording of Deuteronomy 10:12-22 (see text, p. 169).

   Before playing it, divide the class into two listening teams. One team is to listen for evidence that God does deeply love Israel. The other team is to listen for affirmations that reflect God's love for us now.

   You may need to play the recording more than one time.

   Then on the chalkboard develop a two-column chart to make a list of your students' observations.

When whichever of these activities you choose to use is completed, spend time discussing with your class the importance of love in our growth as persons and as Christians. Can "God's love" ever be a substitute for love from others? What does Deuteronomy 6 (see text, pp. 164-167) seem to indicate?

FIGURE VII

**MASLOW'S
HIERARCHY
OF HUMAN
MOTIVATIONS**

SELF
ACTUAL-
IZATION

(the need
to be creative,
to contribute,
to find life
"meaningful")

EGO NEEDS

(the need to "achieve," and
to understand and respect myself)

SOCIAL NEEDS

(the need for "affiliation," to feel accepted,
to be understood and respected by others)

SECURITY NEEDS

(the need to feel safe and secure, to
be free of threat from present or future harm)

PHYSIOLOGICAL NEEDS

(the need for shelter, food, drink, warmth
and other physical comforts and pleasures)

INPUT

Select one or more of the following:

There are a variety of important concepts you might want to build into this class discussion. Here are several from which you may wish to select. But do avoid the temptation to spend much class time in lecture. It's important today that your class members realize that they are loved by God, and that as a result they can become loving. These truths will be communicated best in a sharing rather than lecture atmosphere.

1. You may wish to introduce here Maslow's "hierarchy of needs." This concept has been very significant in much modern thought. It has been developed by Keith Miller (*The Becomers*, Word Books) in its impact for Christians. The basic idea is that until lower-order needs in the hierarchy are met, the person is blocked from growth in higher areas. Maslow's pyramid is shown in Figure 8.

   This theory should not, of course, be presented as though it were revealed truth. At the same time, the insights reflected here can be appreciated and can give us tools for thinking about ourselves in our relationship with God and others.

2. It would be appropriate here to explore John 15 in a mini-lecture (see *probe* 3). Note the parallels.

   ■ Relationship is stressed (15:1-4).

   ■ Discipline is involved (15:5-6).

   ■ God's words are to be in our hearts (15:7-8).

   ■ Love is affirmed (15:9).

   ■ Love experienced demands our response (15:9-15).

   ■ God Himself chose us (15:16).

   ■ Our life-style is to set us off from others round about us (15:17-25).

   ■ God's promised presence with us is full equipment and resource (15:26, 27).

   These are striking parallels which will help to

reinforce your students' awareness that all they read of redemption's story in the Old Testament truly *is* relevant to them today.

IMPACT

Select one or more of the following:

1. Ask each student to select one short passage from Deuteronomy 5—11 that speaks especially to him or her. Give five minutes for the search. Then go around the class and ask each in turn to read the passage he selected and explain why.
2. If you did not begin class with the first *Launching* activity, it would be appropriate to close with it, and to have a time together in prayer.

DESTINY AHEAD

As WE COME TO THE END of this course, you'll want
to decide whether or not to make this the last class,
and use the next class period for an exam. The last
chapter in the text is a study of Moses the man.
Moses has, of course, been the dominant historical
figure during this entire period of the Exodus. I've
refrained from exploring passages which focus on
him and his ministry as we traced the development
of events reported here. In chapter 13 of the text
we draw together much that is revealed about this
man to whom God spoke as a friend, face to face.

You may want to treat the 13th chapter as a
"bonus" for personal enrichment, to be read by individuals. Or you may want to discuss Moses in class
and give your class a take-home exam or skip exam
procedures entirely. Or you may wish to give a
take-home exam now, and use the class time next
week to talk through your students' answers.

Each of these options has its own advantages.

Choose the one best suited to your teaching goals.

LAUNCHING

Select one or more of the following:

Marked (†) items are suitable if you wish to use this class primarily for the personal enrichment and application of truths by your students. Other items are appropriate if you are stressing content mastery or preparation for an examination.

†1. Ask two or three students to read aloud their description of the results for believers today of an uncommitted life (see *personalize* 3). Let these lead into general discussion. (Note that Galatians 5 contrasts the works of the flesh and the fruit of the Spirit, explaining what God seeks to do within the human personality. This might be one clue to the "fruitfulness" of our personalities in comparison to the Old Testament fruitfulness of the land.)

†2. Put a two-column chart on the chalkboard, and ask your students to fill in the parallels they see between the choice of commitment given Israel in this passage and the commitment choice given believers today (*personalize* 2).

3. Begin with an outline of Israel's future (see Input), then work through specific events foretold in these passages. This approach will save time for review and preview for the exam.

INPUT

Select one or more of the following:

†1. Discuss the Deuteronomy 30 evidences that

God is concerned with our heart-response to Him. Such a response will be evidenced by obedience. As we've seen earlier, the same pattern is shown in the New Testament (Jn. 15—last week's study).

2. Put on the board an outline of Israel's history from the death of Moses through the birth of Christ. Do not be too detailed (see Fig. TS 9), but give a framework for historical incidents in which events warned of in the Deuteronomy passage are worked out in reality.

   Build your own lecture from the 28th and 29th chapters of Deuteronomy. But do not spend more than 20 minutes on this discussion.

IMPACT

Select one or more of the following:

†1. Ask each student to write down briefly on a sheet of paper what he sees for himself if his *present* life-style is continued. Then ask each to work with Deuteronomy 30 to see if God is saying anything special to him right now.

2. Give a preview of the exam, especially discussing question types. (See pp. 280-284 of this supplement.)

3. Give a quiz now, especially of the material on the mastery chart (pp. 150, 151). Do not grade it. But let your class know they are and will be responsible for it.

ASSIGNMENT: Before giving the assignment, study the test discussion on pages 276-280. You may

CHART OF ISRAEL'S DESTINY

534
Remnant
return

1450

1400
Conquest

Moses'
death

Malachi
(Last book
in O.T.)

Judges;
decline

1010-930
David/
Solomon
Kingdom

930 Divided

Christ
comes

70 A.D.
Second
destruction
of Jerusalem,
Titus the
Roman,
scattered

Israel (N. Kingdom)

Judah (S. Kingdom)

723
Captured
by Assyria,
scattered

Captured by Babylon, scattered
Destruction of Jerusalem   606/586

FIGURE IX

want to give an essay section of the test to be taken before class—and give the objective part in class.

Or you may simply want to assign the next chapter of the text. Select the approach which will best meet your own objectives in teaching this course.

COMMISSIONED

SHOULD YOU DECIDE TO forego testing and treat this 13th week as a regular class, focus on the lessons your own students have learned from their study of Moses, God's faithful servant.

For a change of pace, make this a discussion (or sharing) class. For this week skip the regular structuring (*Launching, Input, Impact*), and simply start the class off with one or two stimulators. Then let the class process develop freely, perhaps inserting one or more of the focus activities as they seem appropriate.

Here are some possible discussion starters:
1. How do you think Moses felt at the end of his life, looking back over his ministry?
2. What leadership lessons do you think we can learn today from Moses?
3. From your study of Moses, how do you think we should understand "authority"? What does

"having authority" involve? What doesn't it involve?

4. In what ways do you think spiritual leaders today are like Moses? In what ways are they different from Moses?

5. What one lesson from Moses' life do you believe God wants *you* to learn? Why?

6. How responsible do you believe leaders really are for the responsiveness of those that they lead?

Here are some possible focus activities:

1. In class look together at Moses' prayer (Num. 11:11-15). How is this like/unlike our own prayers? What do we learn from this prayer and its response (cf. *Going Deeper*, p. 199)?

2. Examine the incidents in which Moses' humanity and fallibility are particularly in view: Exodus 3, 4; Numbers 11 (see vs. 23), etc. What does this portrait of Moses have to say to us?

TO CONCLUDE:

It should be very valuable both to you and to your class to take time to express personal growth and learning through your study together. So take the last 15 minutes, and have your students write out: "How God has used these books of the Bible in my life." Collect the papers, read them, and later return them. Be sure to write encouraging comments on the papers. This will be meaningful to each class member.

TESTING

Testing has great value both for the teacher and student. For the teacher there is insight into what important principles the students are mastering. For the student there is evidence of growth and learning. In fact, testing should be designed to give just this kind of feedback data to both teacher and learner.

Misuses of testing. At times testing is used for other purposes. Sometimes tests are designed to show up what the student does *not* know. The "almost impossible to pass" test that most of us have experienced does not help the teacher or the student. At other times tests are used primarily as tools of competition. Grading is based entirely on test performance, and so individuals view a test as a contest—and view others as rivals against whom they compete. Whatever may be said for such a philosophy in secular subjects, it is a very bad dimension to build into a Christian learning experience. For spiritual growth we need to learn how to minister to and to cooperate with each other. Competitive attitudes built up by testing approaches are definitely harmful to this vital goal.

These two illustrations make it clear that testing can be misunderstood and misused. When it is misused, its potential benefits will be lost.

Weakness of some testing. There are other ways to lose the benefits of testing as well. Sometimes tests focus on facts and content to the exculsion of meaning. In such cases, all that tests indicate is the ability of individuals to memorize.

The problem with such testing is that when we are dealing with Scripture we want to stress the importance of meaning and application. Bible facts are true, yes. But they are also meaningful. God speaks to us in history and in His revealed Word in order that we might know Him, and in order that our total personalities might be transformed. Thus factual type tests have a very limited value. True, our students must know the facts. But they must also know the message communicated through them, and show awareness of the need for personal response.

The kind of testing which is appropriate for us in Christian education is a testing which probes the attitudes and values and behaviors of our students as well as their possession of information.

We can, in fact, sum up good testing by saying that it provides positive feedback to the student and teachers by giving evidence that growth is taking place in the learner across his whole personality.

The models of possible test approaches provided in this discussion, then, are designed to help you construct tests for this particular series of studies which will help your students realize, "I'm growing!" If you are in a situation where you do grade your students, you will of course use test results to determine part of that grade. But is is very helpful if grading is based on additional factors as well, such as class participation, doing extra work, etc.

In fact, a contract system for grading is something that will help remove the testing part of your program from the competitive realm.

An option. What is a contract approach, and how does it help remove some of the competitive and judgmental overtones of testing? It is announcing to the class at the beginning of a course a basis on which they will be graded which does not rely on the tests that will be given. For instance, I used this approach and set up conditions like these:

1. Everyone is expected to be in class and complete daily assignments.
2. Everyone is expected to take and pass all quizzes and exams, with a minimum score of 75 percent. (Those who do not reach the minimum score will take the test over until they do.)
3. Students who successfully complete the first two requirements will receive a "guaranteed" C. Students who want a higher grade (a B or an A) can earn one by undertaking extra credit work as follows.
4. For a B, complete tests and quizzes with minimum score of 80 percent. Undertake any *four* extra *probe* assignments agreed on between student and teacher, and complete satisfactorily.
5. For an A, complete tests and quizzes with minimum score of 85 percent. (Tests can be re-taken to reach B and A minimums.) Do any eight extra *probe* assignments agreed on between student and teacher, and complete satisfactorily.

By revising the grading structure in this way, no student is competing with others to get his grade. Guidance is still provided by the teacher in terms of helping students select their extra *probe* tasks. Satisfactory work is expected, with low-quality *probe* studies returned to be redone.

Within this framework, the testing itself loses some of the negative associations most testing sometimes has. Tests can be developed to maximize benefits to the learner!

COGNITIVE DOMAIN

Much of testing rightly is designed to disclose what a student does and does not understand. Various mental processes are involved: remembering, recalling, thinking, problem solving, creating, etc. A number of specific tasks can be given to students which will involve these processes and help you—and them—see how much they understand of what the course has contained.

Here are some examples of ways to test for understanding at various levels:

Selecting. A multiple choice or true/false pattern is often adapted to have a student select choices, and thus indicate a knowledge of specific facts. For instance:
(1) Which of the following was not an Israelite:
    (a) Moses   (b) Caleb   (c) Rahab   (d) Miriam
(2) T F Pharaoh was about 80 years old when the young Moses came out of the wilderness to challenge him.

Recall. Often you will want to test for knowledge of facts without providing "clues" in your question. Here are two ways to test for recall:
(1) List three reasons why captivity in Egypt was in

God's plan for Israel. Or, list seven of the ten plagues. Or, list two reasons why the plagues were important parts of God's purposes for Israel.

(2) Reproduce the "Understanding Redemption" chart from chapter 10, but leave a number of items blank. Have your students fill in the blanks.

Classify. Classifying of events or incidents or persons is also a good test of understanding. Here is one way to test on this level.

For each of the following, write:

    A. If the occurrence is best associated with the Law

    B. If the occurrence is best associated with worship

    C. If the occurrence is best associated with disobedience

    D. If the occurrence is best associated with obedience

_____ 1. Israel camps at Sinai.

_____ 2. The Tabernacle plan is given to Moses.

_____ 3. Aaron is ordained as a priest.

_____ 4. Israel is commanded to go into the Promised Land.

_____ 5. The people party while Moses is on Sinai.

_____ 6. Laws concerning the sin offering are explained.

_____ 7. An altar is placed at the entrance to the Tabernacle compound.

_____ 8. An altar of incense is placed before the veil in the Tabernacle.

_____ 9. Levi's sons kill a number of Israelites.

Sequencing. Often several cognitive processes can be combined in a single-question approach. For instance, this one demands both recall and analysis:

(1) Place the following events in correct temporal sequence, and in two sentences explain the significance of that sequence for *any two* events.

> Tabernacle system given
> Law given
> Sacrificial system explained
> Priesthood ordained

Matching. This simple approach also calls for several cognitive processes if developed carefully. For instance, what makes this example of matching so difficult is that in several cases there is more than one "right" answer—but each must be correctly matched for the set to be correct.

(1) Match this set of seven people with the descriptions given by drawing a line between items in Column A and those in Column B.

Column A	Column B
Moses	priesthood
Joshua	Tabernacle service
Caleb	spy
Aaron	military captain
Korah	The Ten Words
Miriam	leprosy
Levi	rebellion

Translation. Other test types measure comprehension of principles and concepts as well as knowledge of facts. Here are two approaches that test comprehension by asking the student to translate a concept expressed in one way to another form.

(1) "The divine doctrine of salvation stresses the fact of man's helplessness as well as God's power and His willingness to intervene on our behalf."
   The above truth is reflected most clearly in:
   (a) God's plagues upon Egypt
   (b) Israel's slavery in Egypt
   (c) The giving of the Law
   (d) The rebellion against Moses

(2) Which statement best expresses the function of the Law in the life of God's Old Testament people?
   (a) The Law defined the believer's life-style.
   (b) The Law shows Israel the way of salvation.
   (c) The Law showed how to respond to God in love and obedience.
   (d) The Law restrained Israel from sin.

Analysis and synthesis. These two higher-order cognitive processes can be tested in various ways, but are best tested using the essay. For instance,

(1) Write an essay about God's purpose in giving the Law, and integrate each of the following: love, standards, character, life-style, faith.

(2) Relate the Law and Grace in a one-page discussion of the Ten Commandments.

(3) Identify and discuss the main issue dealt with in Numbers 11—21.

(4) Select key words to explain the life-style of Israel under the Law—and write a definition of each which will show its significance.

AFFECTIVE DOMAIN

In Bible teaching it is not only important that a person understand Bible truths, but that he respond to them. This includes valuing and applying what is learned in significant ways. Since testing is for the value of the learner as well as the information of the teacher, you'll want to include testing elements which will provide data on the learner's attitudes, values and behavior in response to truth as well as elements measuring his comprehension. There is obviously an overlap between understanding and attitude/response. But both need to be given special attention.

Acceptance of a value. These variations are designed to show both knowledge of the Biblical setting, and personal response to the Scripture messages.

1. For each of the following statements about the believer's life-style, circle *A* if Israel generally *did* demonstrate that quality, *B* if Israel *did not* demonstrate it. Then circle *Y* if you believe you generally do demonstrate this quality now, *Z* if you believe you do not.

284

A B (1) Show thankfulness for God's acts.   Y Z
A B (2) Follow the leader God appointed.   Y Z
A B (3) Complain about wants being unmet.   Y Z
A B (4) Communicate directly with God.   Y Z

2. Rank each of the following values which are taught in Exodus-Deuteronomy as to their importance for a close relationship with God. Then (A) discuss the number one ranked item showing how Israel's behavior either did or did not express this value. Then (B) discuss how your own behavior either does or does not express this same value. Here are the values to rank: trust, obedience, thankfulness, contentment, confidence.

Self-report. A report of specific behaviors that express values is also helpful in evaluating the impact of God's truth on our lives. Here are several ways to measure responsiveness through a self-report of our special behaviors:

1. For each of the following sections of Scripture, circle the one letter key which most accurately describes your behavior:
    A. If you read more than was assigned in the Bible itself
    B. If you read the assigned Bible material carefully and thoughtfully
    C. If you read the assigned Bible material, but superficially
    D. If you read only the textbook, and did not read the Bible itself

    A B C D (a) Exodus 1—4
    A B C D (b) Exodus 5—11
    A B C D (c) Exodus 11—18

2. For each of the messages of this section of the Bible, circle the letter key which best describes your attitude to that message:

  A. Interesting, but not especially relevant
  B. Of vital concern to me personally
  C. Of vital concern to Israel
  D. Led to specific responses to God by me
    A B C D (1) Man needs redemption.
    A B C D (2) God acts to redeem.
    (For more messages, see chart, pp.150,151)

3. Write a brief essay on "the impact of this study of redemption on my own life."

There are many other ways to approach testing. But these illustrations may help you to develop a test for this course which will be meaningful to you and to each of your class members.